Sell By Owner and Save

The Complete Guide to Selling Your Home Without a Real Estate Agent

Michael M. Kloian

Second Edition

H-2 Press

a division of How To LLC

Published by: H-2
a division of How To I
P.O. Box 53
Howard City, MI 4

Copyright© 2002 by Michael M. Kloian

Printed and bound in the United States of America

ISBN # 0-9707346-2-X
Second Edition

Library of Congress Control Number: 2002104206

Kloian, Michael M.
     Sell it by owner and save: the complete guide to selling your
     home without a real estate agent / Michael M. Kloian
     Includes Glossary and Index
     ISBN 0-9707346-2-X (softcover alk.paper)
     1. Real Estate. 2. Business. 3. Finance. 4. How to-self help.

email: publisher@howtollc.com
        author@how2sellbyowner.com

www.howtollc.com

www.sellitbyownerandsave.com

PREFACE

When the project of writing this book began my colleagues wanted to know why I, a real estate broker, was interested in revealing information previously hidden from the average homeowner. They believed that, because of my business expertise, were I to write such a book, it would be a bombshell and they wondered about the impact such a book would have in the "world of real estate."

Over the course of many years in real estate I made it a practice to talk with hundreds of customers, clients and strangers, that crossed my path on issues related to buying and selling real estate. I was especially interested in hearing their stories, good and not so good, including their honest opinions about their *personal* experiences. At the time I made no conscious attempt to amass the information to compile a book of their experiences. Yet, years later, it seemed fitting with what I knew that I could combine this information with the inside story of buying and selling real estate to create a 'book of knowledge' that could assist both buyers and sellers. This was the genesis for a *diary* of notes that eventually led to formulating the outline for this book.

It's no secret that many homeowners would love to save money by selling their own home. Statistics show that one in four homeowners try to sell their own home for various reasons, the most popular being to save the commission. Statistics also indicate many sellers don't sell or they *throw in the towel*. This tells me that by-owner sellers generally lack the knowledge or motivation necessary to see the process to completion, give up and list their home with an agency. It was for this and other reasons that prompted me to undertake this project.

From my own experiences I've learned that the buying and selling public places an extraordinary amount of trust in real estate professionals, and places in their hands the biggest investment of a lifetime, the sale or purchase of their home. Unfortunately, many homeowners had experiences with real estate agents that were disappointing. This, in part, also prompted me to write this book.

There is no doubt that in real estate, as in any profession, there are those whose level of skill or competency exceeds others. Anyone who has ever called tech support for computer or software related problems could relate to this. This also holds true in the medical, legal, technical field and every other industry. Real estate however is one vocation that requires little or no college education, experience or prior skills. Yet we, in the business, find ourselves assisting people with the single largest investment they will make and sometimes doing so cavalierly with little regard to the responsibility placed in our hands.

I don't pretend to believe that this **one** book will change the way the average home buyer or home seller will do business but I do believe the reader will gain a new and unique insight into the world of real estate. It is my hope that you read this book cover to cover.

Michael M Kloian

INTRODUCTION

Selling your home is **not** a matter of "luck." When buying or selling a home, *"timing"* is everything (what happened to location, location, location?). However, possessing *"knowledge or know-how"* is just as important as *"timing."* The *"know-how"* is the inner workings that can effectuate the *"timing."* Without the know-how the effort in capturing timing, in a given situation, may be futile (there are numerous examples throughout this book to illustrate this point). There is no doubt that these **two key ingredients** can lead to success in any selling situation.

"Sell It By Owner and Save" is **not** one of those predictable or generic, *"I've read this and seen this before"* or *"something is missing"* how-to information guides. Often you don't recognize what's missing in a how-to-sell book until you reach a crucial point during your selling experience only to discover that you need answers to serious questions and there's no one to turn to for help.

"Sell It By Owner and Save" is written in simple layman's terms yet with as much detail as necessary for each reader to gain a *thorough* understanding of the *how-to-sell-by-owner* process. The intention of the author is to de-mystify the entire selling process and instruct the reader. This way anyone, regardless of any real estate knowledge or selling skills, will be able to use this valuable information to sell their home, anywhere.

The reward for your efforts will be:

- Thousands of dollars in saved commissions $$$$$$$$$.
- A feeling of great accomplishment, where you are in charge, similar to selling your car for a *fair price* rather than trading it in at a dealership and taking a beating.
- The mere satisfaction that you have overcome the "system"; the system that says you can't do it without "them"; the system that teaches people, when buying or selling, to become dependent on "them".

Your success in selling by-owner depends on many factors such as asking price (in relation to its true market value), condition, location, competition, time of year, exposure to the market, buyer's motivation, your motivation, interest rates, the economy, including your patience and willingness to negotiate or compromise. *"Sell It By Owner and Save"* creates a healthy balance of these dynamics and, coupled with many illustrations and explanations, will walk you through the entire selling process. Also included are many *true* case examples that will be instructive and useful.

If you are motivated to succeed at selling your own home, without a real estate agent, but lack the *"know-how"* then you came to the right place to learn. This book was created for the serious minded by-owner seller. The details in *"Sell It By Owner and Save"* are unmatched. All the information in *"Sell It By Owner and Save"* is from first hand experience. Everything is discussed including Trade Secrets, Little Known Secrets, everything there is to know about how to sell your home by-owner step by step, so you can sell your own home, save money doing so, and earn the pride of accomplishment.

The Publisher

CONTENTS

Part II

SECTION VI Determining your state real estate laws; intricacies of the seller's disclosure statement and sales contract; patent vs. latent defects; more on agency disclosure; city code inspection; who said "shoot all the lawyers", we may need them

Part I

Part II

SECTION VII Who is responsible to pay for which closing costs; sixteen separate expenses are explained in detail; home inspection services; code violations; appraisals; home warranty purchase plans are discussed in detail

SECTION VIII **What to do when a buyer is ready to purchase; how to determine their qualifications; filling out and understanding the sales contract; the good faith deposit; more information on negotiating with your buyer**

SECTION IX   Closing your own sale is easy; title insurance and attorney assistance discussed

SECTION X   The open house myth exposed

SECTION XI   Why do most by-owner sellers throw in the towel and list?; the By Owner Broker; The MLS (multiple listing service) explained

Section I

WHO should and WHO should NOT attempt to sell their home by-owner.

In this section I discuss the pros and cons, advantages and pitfalls, for those attempting to sell their own home. My intention here is to encourage you to realistically assess your suitability to selling your home by owner, to allow you to decide if selling your own home is right for you.

I also discuss the *myths* that some real estate agents may use on by-owner sellers to try to persuade them to "list".

"Disclosure" is introduced in this section.

Part I

WHO SHOULD CONSIDER SELLING BY OWNER

Ask yourself this question. Why do you want to sell by owner? Is it because you want to save the commission or because you've had an unfavorable experience with a real estate company or agent and you've lost faith in them and their ability to deal honestly with you? Or maybe you simply want to prove that you could do it without "them."

You really don't need an answer. All you need is desire, commitment and *know how*. That's all it takes!

If you are confident, secure, not afraid to meet with and talk to a variety of strangers, invite them into your home, be available for appointments, offer documentation (fact sheet, seller's disclosure statement, etc.), fill out a sales contract (optional), discuss the good faith deposit, and if you feel you can adequately explain the buying process to your prospects, then you are a good candidate for selling your own home no matter where you live and no matter what price range your home may fall under.

There are neighborhoods in many cities that are "hot markets" *(see Glossary)* where homes sell quickly because of the location, the neighborhood, the schools, or because the price range of homes is well suited to a large group of buyers. If you live in one of these "hot markets" you are probably already aware of it and stand an excellent chance of selling your home yourself. Most likely you will not need the services of a real estate agent or an attorney. This book should be very helpful in your efforts.

I live in a densely populated rural area, away from the crowded city, where it is more challenging to sell by owner. But it doesn't matter where your home is located if you know which media is best to use to advertise your home. Living in rural areas away from the city may actually increase your chances of selling by-owner since many people are *moving* to these outlying communities. Prices are often much lower further away from the suburbs of a major city, offering prospective buyers more home for the money. Selling may take a bit longer and it may cost extra advertising dollars but the rewards will be the same.

WHAT WILL IT COST TO SELL BY-OWNER?

Selling your own home requires certain expenditures. You should be prepared to pay for things like a quality sign ($25 - $50), brochure box ($20 - $30), flyers, brochures, handouts ($10 - $50), your own personal web site or listing placement fees for the Internet (free - $100), newspaper and home magazine ads ($200-$1,000), and other incidentals.

If you are comfortable with setting aside a certain dollar amount to ensure your success in selling by-owner then you are definitely a candidate for selling your own home. If you are the overly "conservative type" you may find yourself wondering why you've wasted all that money ("Gee, we spent $50 bucks on ads and no one ever came. Do you think we made a mistake"?).

I feel strongly that if you make an honest attempt with the correct approach, based on only one thing, your desire to save the commission, then you should succeed. If this is you, then you certainly qualify to sell your home by owner.

WHO SHOULD NOT ATTEMPT TO SELL BY-OWNER

There are people from all walks of life who may be looking to purchase your home. They may be single, married, unmarried (living together), with or without children, widowed, divorced, heterosexual, homosexual, disabled, people from every religious, racial or ethnic background, whose convictions and beliefs may differ from yours. You will need to look beyond how they are dressed, length of their hair, color of their skin, their mannerisms and any quirky "personality" traits you may find awkward or strange. Don't forget, you may seem strange to them. There are some homeowners who have *no fear* of strangers and others who are extremely cautious or *fearful* of strangers.

My advice to you if you are:

- skittish about taking phone calls without first checking your caller ID
- jumpy, nervous or alarmed by outside or inside noises
- afraid to answer the door unless you see identification or know the person
- worried or afraid that a neighbor may be watching you
- fearful of being robbed or your home vandalized, or living in a high crime neighborhood
- fearful about showing your home because you live alone
- unsure about answering specific questions related to your home; dealing with strangers; making and keeping appointments; drafting or filling out documents (optional); handling objections or asking a stranger questions.

If any of these reflect you then you may want to *reconsider* selling your home by-owner. The balance of this selling guide will explain in greater detail the kinds of things that may be expected of you once you decide to sell your home by-owner.

SALESMANSHIP AND SECURITY

Much like selling your own car you will need to meet with potential buyers, talk to them, make sense (in other words sound somewhat knowledgeable), present documentation and handle yourself in a professional and courteous manner. You will also need to parade strangers through your home at various hours of the day or on weekends. Many of these prospects are no doubt trustworthy and forthright citizens. A few, however, may not be. If this makes you nervous in any way, *do not* attempt to sell your own home. Let a professional handle it.

THE MYTHS

One argument some real estate agents use to coerce by-owner sellers into listing their homes is the *"danger"* theory. Real estate agents know how to play on the emotions and inexperience of by-owner sellers. They may say that allowing strangers into your home poses potential dangers or problems. While there may be a little truth to this such problems are isolated and minimal. However, I will relate a recent personal experience to illustrate that sometimes such problems do exist.

I sell new homes and live in a model home (my own personal home) that I demo in a new housing development. Over the course of a year I have had hundreds of visitors come through my model home, far more than you'll ever experience. Many are sincere and looking to build a new home or they may simply be "house shopping." Others are time wasters, "looky-loo's" *(see Glossary)* and "gawkers" I call them, people who love to look with no intention ever of buying, and still fewer, if any, may be thieves or crooks.

On one occasion I escorted a couple around, and watched them closely as they toured my model home. They seemed less interested in the home than its contents. They looked through the closets, at the clothes, what was on the shelves, the dresser, the decor and whatever else seemed to catch their eyes. I was not overly suspicious but their behavior certainly was. However, I remained alert and watchful. Let's face it, yes, it's possible, you may also get one or two of these *"buyers"* coming to your home. I say this not to scare you but to alert you to that possibility and to advise you to remain alert.

However, some real estate agents constantly exaggerate such problems and use them to persuade by-owner sellers to list their home, warning that it will be safer to list with an agency because they "screen" their buyers. However, is this really true?

Should you find yourself face to face with an agent, and the opportunity, the questions to ask are:

- what exactly is their screening process?
- do they really 'screen' the buyer?
- do they really check each prospect before working with them?
- do they verify the buyer's employment?
- do they know what *scam* a buyer may have been involved with in the past?
- do they know if a prospect has a criminal record?

Their argument claims that by-owners may be letting into their homes "unqualified buyers" or "strangers" who may be dishonest and have hidden motives. By "unqualified" they may imply that the potential buyers have bad credit and once they contract to buy a home they may not "qualify." Or perhaps the buyer has a good income but they also have too many other debts, which reduces their ability to borrow sufficient funds to make a purchase. Or is it possible that the buyer may not have two nickels to rub together? Is the agent empowered to dig into a prospective buyer's bank account records or perform a credit check? Or can it mean that these strangers are merely posing as potential buyers? Will the agent run a background check to see if they have a criminal record? The answer? No way!

Once you think this through you realize that anyone can pose as a home-buyer. There may not be hard statistics to offer on theft of items that occur as a result of showing strangers through a home but I'm certain if such acts were to happen, they could happen to anyone, either to a by-owner seller or an agent-listed home. Nevertheless, it's best to err on the side of caution.

It's always wise to leave valuables safely tucked away, unexposed in a well hidden or secure area of your home. Tucked away does not mean under the pillow or mattress. Will some people steal personal items if left unattended? Possibly! Every department store has thieves walking around all the time yet merchandise is constantly exposed. Who knows what thieves look like or who they are? They could be anybody.

Here is another example. Several days after some people toured my model home, I discovered in the basement an open box of personal collector items that belonged to my son, items of some modest value. It appeared that someone had rifled through the box and helped themselves to some items. I have no idea who it was, when it happened, or how many items were missing. I didn't notice the open box until later. It was clearly my mistake for not escorting the buyers into the basement. Never did I think someone would find a sealed box, open it and steal contents from it. THIS CAN HAPPEN TO YOU! Now, as a standard practice, I escort each couple as they tour my model home. If they go in separate directions I stay with the one who is headed for the bedroom. I then monitor how long the partner is in the basement then proceed to join them.

DISTRACTIONS

If a family arrives at my model home and children dash in different directions I stop them and ask the parents to keep their children close-by while viewing my home. A misbehaved child in a stranger's home is another topic. I've seen kids do everything from sliding down my stairs to jumping on the couch when they arrive. This distraction may be just the opportunity a thief is counting on. One cannot predict if theft will take place in such circumstances but it's much safer to hide or completely remove all valuables during a showing, especially during an open house where you have opened the *flood gates* for people to tour your home with no knowledge of who they are or where they come from.

PART II

DISCLOSURE - HONESTY IS THE ONLY POLICY

Placing a *FOR SALE BY OWNER* sign on the lawn is the first step to selling your own home, and it's the easiest. When showing your home, you must be honest with prospective buyers. This means that when asked you will need to disclose *(see Glossary)* what is wrong with your home, or what was wrong and corrected. This means the exact month and year when the furnace was installed, and by whom. Statements like "we replaced the furnace a few years ago" don't cut it. A *few years ago* could mean two or three years ago in a buyer's mind. In a seller's mind a few years ago may mean five or ten years, making the furnace older rather than newer.

That is one reason why many states have passed legislation forcing the seller to disclose to the buyer any and all known defects *(see Glossary - patent and latent defects)* the seller is aware of. This is something you should document in writing in order to forestall a buyer's objections or erase from the buyer's mind any hint that your home is not worthy of consideration. Where there are such disclosure laws they apply to everyone. Even when selling your home by-owner you are **not** exempted from "disclosure." In Section VI seller's disclosure is discussed in detail.

If you live in one of the states that do not have mandatory disclosure laws please consider this: telling the buyer what was wrong with the home and how it was corrected tells the buyer you're honest and shows you are a caring and responsible homeowner. Not telling the buyer you have cracks in the basement walls that may leak periodically during a very heavy rain, though you can't see them, since they are well hidden behind paneling, is not a good idea. They **will** find out eventually. Once a hidden or undisclosed defect is discovered your buyer will then assume there are other problems and that you are less than truthful concerning other aspects of the home. Selling your home by-owner **does not** diminish your responsibility to deal honestly and fairly with potential buyers.

One tactic real estate agents may use to discourage buyers from seeking out by-owner homes is to convince them it is *safer* to work with agents rather than deal directly with owners because by-owner sellers may not disclose all the defects, insinuating buyers are better protected if they deal with a real estate agent. This is incorrect since owners, whether their homes are listed-by-agent or for-sale-by-owner, **must** by law disclose any and all known defects if they live in a state where disclosure is mandatory.

Keep in mind that your buyers have a right to hire a home inspection service, so long as it is mutually agreed upon in writing, and most likely they will if your home is older than 15-20 years. If your buyers have ever been to a realty office or have used the services of buyers' agents, or discussed with them the intricacies of buying a home, they may already be aware of the importance of a home inspection. The inspection service **will** disclose defects to the buyer, with or without your help. The use of inspection services, or the right of the buyer to hire one, is stated in almost every Sales Contract used today. Only an uninformed buyer, or novice, will ignore this aspect of the purchase process. We will discuss the sellers' disclosure statement and inspection companies later since these topics are very important and worthy of further discussion.

PATIENCE IS MORE THAN A VIRTUE

You will also need to be patient, very patient. More often than not, despite the hype created by some selling manuals, selling by-owner may take longer than listing with an agent to sell your home. Why? Simply because your exposure to the market is limited by the kind of advertising you use, which may be restricted by your budget, whether you use the Internet, a sign in the front yard, flyers posted in various locations, or ads in newspapers and home magazines.

There are many by-owner sellers who sell their homes in a week, two weeks, or three weeks. Yet, it isn't realistic to expect to sell so quickly. If it happens, it's great. But, I wouldn't count on it. There's no magic formula for selling quickly. If I were to tell you to run two ads, do this, do that, raise or lower your price several thousand dollars, and you will sell your home and you don't, you would think my advice is unreliable. For this reason I offer no hype or exaggerations.

Listing your home with a real estate agent who participates in a multiple listing service is also no guarantee you will sell any quicker. However, because your home is not in the MLS (multiple listing service - see *Glossary*), which is discussed in Section XI, your actual market time may be longer than you anticipate. Sometimes, this can actually work for you, but sometimes also against you.

This can work for you if a real estate agent drives by your FSBO (for sale by owner) home with a client to show a nearby property they found through the MLS and they see your professional FSBO sign (not the cheesy hardware store sign for $4.99 taped to a stick and thrown in the ground at an obscure angle). And if you have a box of brochures attached to your quality looking sign they may be inclined to stop and grab a brochure. If curiosity is a driving force and your home looks appealing, the buyer may even ask the realty agent about your home.

However, some agents tend to misinform their buyer-clients since their information on any given FSBO home is often scanty. If buyers are from the area and truly interested they will probably return without the agent to inquire about your home, as often happens. Unfortunately, some buyers place their complete trust in an agent only to be controlled and manipulated, believing anything the agent says. This *"trust and control"* is one aspect of real estate business practices that I find regrettable for it gives unfair and unwarranted advantage to agents who may not be necessarily honest with their clients.

I'll give you one example of the use of "trust" and "control" that recently happened to me. I advertise new home construction and undeveloped lots on a local real estate channel in a nearby city. My advertising representative had visited a realty office to sell advertising and mentioned our name as clients. She discovered from talking with the agent that a potential buyer had inquired about our homes with the agent instead of calling us directly on our 1-800 number. The agent, *being in control* of the situation and the buyer, made a comment as to why the buyer would want to live *so far* from the city, thus planting seeds of doubt in the buyer's mind. The agent then said that something *must be wrong* with our homes since our prices were so low, casting even more doubt in this unsuspecting buyer's mind. As a result of these comments, this agent was able to sway the buyer by saying whatever was necessary to discourage the buyer from any future interest in our homes.

Some real estate agents may exaggerate or withhold information in order to sway buyers or direct them to other properties. In short, they want to retain buyers to make their own sale. It is unfortunate but true that many people can be led around like sheep. They can be easily misled and ill-advised as soon as they place their complete trust in a 'professional.' Unfortunately, such practices are common among some agents, although certainly not most.

Typical comments agents make to clients may be, "the reason they are selling by-owner is they wouldn't list their home with us," or, "the reason we can't give you any information on that home is that those people are unreasonable" or "they are asking way too much for their home, and, by the way, there may be a foundation problem." Unfortunately many buyers are gullible and may be duped by such agents and these comments go unchallenged.

The Best Time to Sell

You should approach selling your home intelligently, meaning that you set a time frame of three months or longer, depending on your location and your personal circumstances, whatever you feel comfortable with. You should start early in the year, and don't select the slower months of the year, which is traditionally winter. Start in March, April or early summer when you will increase your chances of selling, since there are more buyers shopping for homes during these months. Offering 30 days or less for the buyer to occupy your home after closing also enhances its salability. Buyers dislike waiting 60 or 90 days to occupy a home after closing.

Homes sell all year round and at times that are often unpredictable. I once sold a home by-owner (yes, even real estate brokers can sell by-owner) on New Year's Eve and the buyer presented an offer only hours before midnight.

Your home can sell any time, any month, although there are *peaks* and *valleys* to a real estate buying season. **Exposing your home to the public and marketing your home consistently are the keys to success.**

How Long Will it Take to Sell?

If you are in a hurry to sell for a number of reasons, or because of special circumstances, then you should not consider selling by-owner, unless, of course, you live in a market area that is in high demand where the average market time is one month or less. Offering your home several thousand dollars below market value will, of course, enhance the prospects of a sale but it will not guarantee that you will sell as quickly as needed. Depending on the person some buyers may view this as seller desperation and may mistakenly believe there is something wrong with your home or misjudge your circumstance.

One example of problems you may encounter that could affect the time frame for selling your home by owner may be this: You and your family have been looking for a new home for about a year and now found one you wish to purchase. This is the home of your dreams at a price you find hard to pass up. Your existing home however is not yet for sale. You could purchase the new home by using a contingency clause *(see Glossary)* in the sales contract that stipulates you sell your home first before closing on the new home purchase, providing the owner is willing to accept these terms. Or, you could approach the bank for a mortgage to secure your purchase outright, thereby having two mortgages, one on your existing home and one for the new home. You can then make your offer to purchase the home without a contingency clause.

There are two possible scenarios for this hypothetical example:

Scenario **#1**

You proceed to purchase the new home and discover that the bank will give you a mortgage loan and will also lend you money for the required down payment by giving you a "bridge" loan *(see Glossary)*, money borrowed against your existing house. So now, faced with two mortgage payments over the next several months, or longer, you are under pressure to sell as quickly as possible. You are also under pressure to get **X** amount of dollars after selling your existing home so you can pay off two debts, your existing mortgage and the bridge loan.

You may also be faced with a *contingency loan approval* from the bank, which could jeopardize your plans. The contingency approval from the bank states they will lend you the money to purchase the new home only if you sell and close your existing home first. Some lenders may require that sellers sell and close their existing home before finalizing any new transaction. This depends upon your qualifications, which can change everything.

Two very real problems arise from this first scenario:

    A) the need to sell quickly can pose a real problem if you plan to sell your home by-owner since the time frame in which you must

24

sell depends on several factors that may be out of your control;

B) trying to get the exact amount of money you need from your existing home to satisfy **both** debts, your existing mortgage and the bridge loan, can be tricky if you have overcommitted to another purchase. In other words, you would like to net a certain dollar amount after selling your existing home but fail to consider your existing home's *fair market value, (see Glossary)* which may be lower than you estimated. You may have also forgotten to calculate your true net proceeds after all expenses have been paid from the sale of your existing home.

Now you have placed yourself in the proverbial box of having to sell for a certain dollar amount that you may not actually get. I have seen people do this time and again. The disappointment can be crushing at the time owners sell their home and discover they can't get for their existing home the price they had hoped for and expected. In other words, they needed to sell for X amount in order to net $40,000 at closing when they should really be netting only around $35,000 to reflect actual market value *(see Glossary)*. Your need to net a specific dollar amount to satisfy certain debts you are committed to paying off has little or nothing to do with the "fair market value" of your property.

This wish or "dream" to squeeze a buyer into paying more for your home simply because you need more cash to complete another purchase is risky, unfair and unrealistic. If you sit back hoping some unintelligent, unsuspecting buyer will walk through your door and pay you more than your home is worth then you will be the fool once you sell your home and the bank appraisal comes in lower than the sale price. You will be disappointed and your buyers will be glad since, if the loan is not approved, they do not have to proceed with the transaction. In short, your deal will be dead and it will be your undoing.

If you try to sell your existing home by-owner for one month and don't succeed and end up closing on the new house you now own two homes along with two mortgage payments. If the market turns sour for whatever reason you will find yourself wishing you hadn't bought the new home before selling your existing home. Or, because of time constraints, you may decide to place your existing home in the hands of a realty company that nets you even less money than you could have gotten from selling by-owner. Worse yet, you end up selling your existing home several thousand dollars below market value just to sell quickly and you end up paying many thousands of dollars in commission in addition to taking a loss.

My advice here is very practical. I'm not suggesting you avoid the purchase of the new home before selling your existing home. If you qualify for two loans and are comfortable with the notion of making two mortgage payments then finding a new home before selling your existing home can be an advantage. What you need to avoid is having to sell your home quickly for less than market price just to avoid multiple payments or to meet a specific time frame in a contingency clause. Being desperate to sell is an emotional *pressure cooker* that buyers may discern and may then try to take advantage of during negotiations. There are solutions to this in the next section when we discuss how to establish the fair market value of your home.

Scenario **#2** (for the hypothetical example above):

You found a new home you wish to purchase and have already approached the owners to buy it on the contingency that you sell your home first (to avoid the bridge loan and dual payments), and you enter into a written agreement. The "contingency clause" (*see Glossary*) will hold the new home purchase for a designated period of time, locking in the sale price and terms, allowing you an opportunity to sell your home before *committing*. The contingency clause also allows the sellers of the new home to continue marketing their home. In the event they find another buyer you, the first buyer, will be allowed a certain number of days (typically three) within which you must either remove the "contingency clause" and proceed with the sale or back out of the deal without forfeiting your earnest money deposit *(see Glossary)*.

Now that you've succeeded in securing a purchase contract for your new home for a short duration, utilizing the "contingency clause," you plan to sell your existing home by-owner, something you failed to tell the seller. You decide not to list your home with an agent to save on the commission, which, if successful, will net you more money. You also expect to sell your home in a month or less. Unless you live in a hot, fast moving market this may simply not happen.

The unnecessary anxiety you have placed on yourself may be just the ticket to the nut house. A worse case scenario is you may lose out on buying the new home if you don't sell and close your existing home in the time frame necessary to save your new home transaction from falling apart. If the home you are attempting to purchase is truly your "dream home" then buying it by using a contingency clause that stipulates you must sell your existing home first makes no sense. You were probably better off with two loans, two payments, and taking your chances at selling quickly.

Handling your existing home this way will certainly bring disappointment if you don't sell it in time to satisfy the contingency. You will lose your new home purchase, become discouraged, and you may give up selling and stay miserable in a house you no longer want to live in or have outgrown. Worse yet, this may place a very heavy burden on your relationship with your partner or on your emotions.

PLAN TO SELL EARLY

In order to avoid this predictable mess and prevent the frantic pressure of having to sell quickly you must plan selling by-owner well in advance. There is nothing wrong with looking for a new home before or during the process of selling your home by-owner. I see no problem with negotiating to purchase the home of your dreams then selling your existing home by-owner. I'm merely pointing out some of the pitfalls of selling your home by-owner should you find yourself in any of the situations I mentioned. Also, its not that I lack confidence in your ability to sell by-owner, its just that I have seen this situation repeatedly and I know how to avoid such problems.

I will close this *chapter* with this final pearl: There is a buyer for every home. There is no home that cannot be sold. The only real question is how long it will take. There is no solid answer to this question. It's only a matter of when, not if. Over time I have witnessed the most difficult homes sell and if there is any principal worth repeating its this one - have patience.

Who then will save the commission? The seller, the buyer, or both? This is a question we will explore and discuss in the next section.

Section II

This section will discuss the two most important items: PRICE and TERMS, and will show you.....

- HOW to estimate your home's fair market value, WHO to turn to for help in this process, and HOW to tell if your home is worth more or less than your neighbor's.
- HOW to prepare your home for sale so you can get the highest possible price.
- HOW to tell the difference between a buyer's market and a seller's market.
- HOW to market your home successfully in good times or in not so good times.

I also discuss the whole point to selling your own home, and that is to save the commission.

Part I

PRICE

The **first** thing you must do before putting your home up for sale is to estimate and verify the correct, *"fair market value" (see Glossary)* of your home, condominium or other type of property (resort, timeshare, vacant land, etc). This could be done from a new appraisal *(see Glossary - appraised value)*, performed by a certified, residential fee appraiser, or from a slightly older appraisal if you've refinanced your home within the past year (which might now be lower or higher than your current market value), or a CMA, (comparative market analysis) performed by a real estate agent. The CMA *(see Glossary)* will show recent sales data of comparable homes in your immediate market area and may be **the best** free source of information (I'll tell you below how to get this information). The certified appraisal may be more accurate and reliable because a third, disinterested and unbiased party, is performing the work for a fee.

You will need to know your competition. Typically, this would be homes for sale in your immediate neighborhood or surrounding area, which are similar in style, size and quality to yours. Knowing the price these homes are "listed" for is necessary for estimating your *'fair market value'* asking price. The reason I emphasize 'fair market value' (*see Glossary*) is to reinforce the importance of establishing an accurate price for your home so prospective buyers, familiar with the price of homes in your area, will be willing to pay your asking price, or just below your asking price, and not be turned away. This price must be substantiated at the time you place your home for sale by-owner so that when the home is sold the buyer's loan will not be refused during the mortgage process due to a lower difference in the home's appraisal.

One reason why so many homeowners choose to sell by-owner is that they believe the suggested selling price offered by a real estate agent is too low. Ironically, a common mistake many homeowners make is pricing their home above market value because of fears they may be underpricing it. While this is natural, a cursory look at prices in your market area will prevent this oversight.

After establishing an approximate value for your home you will then need to compare your home's features with that of the competition. If the homes in your neighborhood are similar to yours, and are listed properties, then you may consider setting your price equal to or just under the highest listed price, provided your home is comparable in size, features, quality of construction, and condition. For example, suppose there are several "like kind" homes within a ten block radius. One home, two blocks away, exactly like yours, is loaded with every amenity including a fireplace and central air-conditioning. Your home, in excellent condition, 'shows well', (clean, neat, good condition, with a good floor plan) is priced the same, yet lacks a fireplace and central air-conditioning. The asking price of your home should be several thousand dollars less than the home two blocks away. If both homes were priced the same and showed with equal appeal, in so far as floor plan, lot size and other similar features, and a buyer were to see both homes (and they will), which home do you think they would consider buying first? The home with more amenities or the one with fewer?

It may seem reasonable at first to price your home the same as your competition down the street but does that make economic sense? I can already hear your argument: "They can always make us an offer." But, dear owner, real estate doesn't work that way. You need to be one step ahead of your competition. Yes, they can always make you an offer but they also might not. Maybe you should be proactive and consider helping buyers in advance by pricing your home "right." It's very important to know your competition before selling your home. It's worth the little time it takes to check this out.

On the other hand, once you learn that the home "down the street" just sold then it may be reasonable to ask the same price as the "sold home" now that it has been removed from the market. Your home may very well be the only home for sale within several blocks. This is good!

Consider this: let's assume, in this hypothetical example, that the market is sluggish because of interest rates, fuel prices, the economy, whatever the reason. The market is not as "fast moving" as it was a year ago or earlier in the year. Now, in your neighborhood, homes seem to be selling every 60 to 90 days, and there are four similar homes for sale in a ten block radius. This means there will be a limited number of buyers approaching your immediate area. This prospect, no doubt, will pursue purchasing a home offering more amenities for the best possible price.

In order to attract that buyer to your property the price should not only be competitive but better than the competition, especially since your home is for sale by-owner. In this example you must make it very attractive to draw in as many prospects as possible. Even if your price was only a smidgen lower it may be enough to entice that one buyer into looking your way, especially if your home's amenities are comparable to other 'like kind' properties nearby. You will have the edge, enough so that the buyer may consider your home over your competition simply because you are priced right.

Also, keep in mind, because you are selling by-owner, you have more room to play with the price because of the commission other home owners are forced to pay. You are now in the unique position of probably selling first, instead of sitting on the market with an attitude, wondering why no one is buying. If you were to list your home with an agent your chances of selling any sooner wouldn't necessarily improve. Your home may still take 60 to 90 days to sell, even if priced below the competition. As a by-owner seller you now have a serious advantage over your competition. Now that you realize this fact you need to put a plan in motion in order to implement this benefit.

One of the *traditional* problems with by-owner sellers is that they tend to expect higher prices for their homes than listed homes. One reason may be because by-owner sellers lack confidence in agents' "price advice" on their homes. When homeowners see a 'for sale' sign go up, then a 'sold' sign attached only two days or two weeks later they may think the price on that home was set too low. For this, and other reasons, they sometimes think a higher asking price seems justified for their home. As if to say, "since homes are selling that fast and for that price maybe we could get more and still sell relatively quickly." In some instances this may be true, especially in those "hot market" areas we will be discussing throughout this book. Generally, however, it's not. These assumptions are often wrong and costly.

Customarily, by-owner sellers ask for more money because they believe their home is worth more, despite what the market dictates. Real estate agents understand how *greed* works against the by-owner seller. They know it's only a matter of time until the by-owner seller, with the overpriced home, comes around. Their hope is that you stay *greedy* and that your home doesn't sell. They know that one day you will give up and list your home and the price then will be in line with the market or it just won't sell. It's at that moment when frustration builds and you lose faith in your ability to sell by-owner. Then when you, out of frustration, "list" your home with an agent and sell it, and pay the *outrageous* commission, you end up taking a beating and coming out of the deal with far less than you anticipated. Why? All because you asked more for your home than the market could bear. The objective here is to price your home according to the market value in your area and to sell it.

PRICE IT RIGHT

The purpose of the above is that, should you encounter a problem selling your home, I want you to see that, in some cases, you may be the cause of your own failure. The point to all of this is that you need to understand *price protocol*. If you don't, forget what others have to say and do your own thing, because you will anyway. If, in a prior selling experience with an agent, you believe you were *burned* by an agent underpricing or underselling your previous home, then it's understandable that you would want to ask more for your home to avoid the *same mistake*. However, you should put aside previous disappointments and stick with tried and true methods that work and not do what you think *might* work merely to compensate for a prior experience.

Remember this about potential buyers. The more "market knowledgeable" they are the easier it is to deal with them when it comes to the value and price of your home. If they have just begun their search for a home you will need to hand them something tangible that shows your price is in line with your market area but allow them some time to discover this on their own. Very few prospects buy the first home they see unless they are "market knowledgeable" and ready, willing, and able to make the purchase. The burden of proof rests with you since you are acting as your own agent. That's why it's best to be prepared.

One of the things I found interesting, yet disappointing, as a real estate broker was helping homeowners establish a fair market value for their home even though I knew instinctively they had no intention of listing with me. They, like many, were just using an agent to establish a fair market value for selling their home by-owner or were substantiating their home's value with another agent. And for good reason. It is very important to get more than one opinion.

As I mentioned, homeowners in general (not only by-owner sellers) have a reputation for inflating the value of their homes. Seldom do we find homeowners asking an agent to lower the price of their home. It is widely believed among real estate professionals that a FSBO home is generally overpriced. Real estate professionals believe this is the one reason why you have chosen to become a FSBO. Because of this, they believe by-owner sellers will ultimately not succeed. For this reason they spend hundreds, if not thousands, of dollars on seminars to learn the latest tactics on how to persuade by-owner homes to ultimately list. These training sessions purport to have *proven techniques* to bring these hard to list by-owner homes under the control of the 'professional.'

PRICE GUIDANCE

Few owners understand the critical importance of placing the correct market value *price-tag* on their home. Some arbitrarily add $20,000 to the price of their home for the pool they installed five or ten years ago, or $20,000 for the new kitchen remodeling job from last year, or $10,000 for finishing their basement twenty years ago or $3,000 for the new roof, etc., etc. Although these improvements certainly add value to the home they do not necessarily justify, dollar for dollar, a higher asking price.

The replacement of windows, doors, carpets, etc., or general upkeep of the home are enhancements to a home and may encourage buyers to purchase your home. A well maintained home always gets **top dollar.** That may be the very reason why a neighbor around the corner got so much money for a similar home. Conversely, a lower priced similar home in the neighborhood may indicate a poorer condition or other problems not generally known so be careful not to price your well maintained home in line with or below those that need TLC (tender-loving-care, *see Glossary*).

The in-ground or above-ground pool may be a plus or a negative factor. This depends on the buyer's viewpoint and needs, not yours. Your input will be helpful in answering the buyer's questions related to the pool's upkeep and costs. Without having any knowledge of those facts a buyer may think the pool is a burden or an added expense not worth taking on and may arbitrarily pass on purchasing your home because of their lack of knowledge. Telling prospects the costs of maintenance and up-keep of your pool may be a wiser choice than allowing them to leave your home second guessing.

I once sold a home where the seller was asked by the buyer, as part of the negotiation, to fill in the cement pool and cover it with dirt to create a larger backyard for his family. As strange as it may seem the seller was happy to accommodate the buyer. I've seen homes with beauti-fully landscaped backyards that had no room for children to play. Be-lieve it or not buyers with children often look for backyards with room to roam, not ponds or bonsai trees. Of course, if you have both, all the better your chances of attracting buyers.

The new kitchen or room addition will certainly help a home's appear-ance but it is unrealistic to believe you will recoup all your expenses for such improvements. Worse yet is when a homeowner, upon hearing through the local grapevine, that a similar home around the corner just sold for some ridiculous higher price, then proceeds to adjust the price. Usually, these rumors are just that, unfounded rumors. If you hear such rumors check them yourself at the Office of The Register of Deeds where the *Warranty Deed* was recorded. The Warranty Deed confirms the date of the transaction and shows the actual sale price. You can also call the County Equalization Department or the Assessor's Office to see if a *Prop-erty Transfer Affidavit* has been filed. This document may indicate how the home was financed, any special terms, such as an owner carried 1st or 2nd mortgage, as well as any other considerations, such as closing costs paid for by the seller, furnishings, appliances or other items that may have been included with the sale and were part of the transaction.

The *Property Transfer Affidavit* is usually completed at the time of closing or may be sent to both buyer and seller after the property is sold and the Warranty Deed is recorded. It confirms and verifies information surrounding the sale, including price, terms, and any special considerations. *Special considerations* exist when a seller adds several thousand dollars to the selling price or has paid several thousand dollars directly to the buyer at closing to help with closing or mortgage costs. Even with these documents you may not know all the facts of the sale. [See below on how to find undisclosed information]

Neighbors are notorious for bragging about getting X amount of dollars for their homes. They do so to *save face* with friends and neighbors. This happens all the time. No one wants others to know how much they *really* sold their home for. Sellers usually want neighbors to think they got top dollar for their home and so they pad the price and *feed* the rumor.

Worse than rumors is a "nosy neighbor" who seems to know more than you do when it comes to placing a value on your home. Do yourself a favor, be polite yet prepared to ignore your neighbor completely. If you don't you may put stock into what your neighbor says and end up with your home still on the market for what will seem forever at a price that is unreasonably high.

THE PRICE IS RIGHT GAME

Prospective buyers are reluctant to negotiate on overpriced homes. Put yourself in their shoes for a moment. They find a home (your home) they like for $150,000 only to find similar homes selling for $140,000 in the same neighborhood. Do you honestly believe they are going to make you an offer $10,000 below your asking price? They may feel they would be insulting you with an offer as low as $140,000, yet the lower price may be perfectly in line with the fair market value of like-kind homes. How would you react to an offer of $10,000 under your asking price? Wouldn't you feel they were trying to take advantage of you? Or is it your belief that they may want your home so bad that they will offer you $145,000 to $148,000, thus allowing you to sell above fair market value.

A grossly overpriced home usually sits on the market until the price is lowered. And when you do adjust the price lower, you will find that you will have to re-market your home since all the original buyers were *scared* away. This equates to more money being shelled out for advertising and plenty of precious market time lost in vain, unless, that is, you were in no hurry to sell and were merely "testing the waters," so to speak.

Learn from others who have already gone that route and price it right to begin with. Otherwise, when and if the day comes that you list your home with an agent, the price of your home will be set to the correct market price anyway, and you could have been there months earlier, sold your home and gone, and saved commission money you now lost because you didn't sell by-owner at the right price. You may also be making many more months of large house payments than expected, which in turn is costing you even more money. The eternal cliché "time is money" is fully applicable to a real estate transaction. I cannot stress too strongly the importance of offering your home at *fair market value*, not a penny more or a penny less. The point is to place the right price on the home that will attract buyers to your home and not chase them away.

DETERMINING THE VALUE OF YOUR HOME

The best way to determine the fair market value of your home is to see what homes in your area have been selling for over the past several months. If you live in a "hot market" you may need to adjust your price upwards or rely on property sale prices 30 days old or less. Remember that *asking price* is different from *selling price*. You can track home prices in your area long before you offer your home for sale. This will serve as a starting point.

Simply call the real estate office that has homes listed in your area and ask them the price and amenities. If a home that you're comparing has a 'sold' sign ask what the home was listed for, what it sold for and under what terms. If they probe or refuse to give you the information tell them you live in the neighborhood and may be selling in the future and want to track sales in your area. If they attempt to pry and ask personal questions you don't wish to answer tell them anything to *quench the thirst*. Real estate people can be very inquisitive.

Their information is public and should be given out freely. They know why you're asking and may assume you plan to sell your home. If they suggest you make an appointment for a free personalized market analysis of your home then you may wish to consider their offer. It may be to your benefit.

How to Establish Fair Market Value

I suggest that you contact at least three real estate agents and ask for a free market analysis, or opinion of value, preferably in writing, and preferably in detail. This may include a simple computer printout of 3 bedroom, 2 bath one-story homes, having features similar to yours, with similar square footage, or it may include a written CMA (see Glossary) showing a breakdown and difference in square footage and features between sold homes. The more professional the agent the more thorough the information that will be presented to you. Only an amateur will be poorly prepared.

Agents will display a broad range of opinions and values. This is to be expected. For example, if your home's value is $140,000, you may receive a price from one agent for $150,000, from another for $145,000, and yet another for $142,500. Many agents would love to quote a higher price just to pull an owner into the listing. They know the owner likes to hear the cash register ring loudly. They may be convincing and may try to *prove*, in writing, that your home will sell for a higher amount. Be leery of agents who seem adamant. This may just be a ploy to list your home for a higher price knowing they will only return in a few weeks, or months later, to lower the price and bring it in line with market value.

Their opinions in general, however, could be helpful in establishing a price for your home by taking the average asking price of comparable homes then taking the average selling price of what they actually sold for. This will give you an estimated asking price range you should be asking for your home and the average selling price will show you what you can expect to actually receive for your home. The two figures, asking and selling, are seldom, if ever, the same.

A buyer will always attempt to negotiate a price lower than the asking price. For this reason it is critical to the outcome of your final sale not to overprice the true value of your home by more than 2% to 3%, which places it nearer its market value yet allows for negotiation. No one should be expected to pay full price for a home unless the original price is so good it leaves little or no room to barter.

In some locations throughout the country certain markets are so "hot" that buyers actually place bids on properties above the asking price just to secure the purchase. You will find this information on the CMA or the computer print out provided to you by an agent. This information is critical to understand your market area. Miscalculating can cost you thousands of dollars or many months of wasted market time.

LOWER THAN NORMAL SELLING PRICES

What is also important to understand when you see homes selling way below their asking price is 'why.' It could mean that the owners chose to take a loss due to personal problems. CMA information can be sketchy, in the absence of first hand knowledge. A complete breakdown showing more detail is best. A very low selling price may indicate a fire sale, i.e. divorce, a must move (where sellers purchased another home and must sell their home fast), relocation, or it may mean the home was in disrepair and the buyer and seller allowed for a "cushion" or an adjustment for the replacement of costly items.

Verifying such information will be necessary if you wish to ask more for your home than lower priced ones. **Don't rely only on a computer print out that has little or no detailed information.** One tact is to look at the written information or remarks on the MLS print out, the actual listing information card for the home, and drive by the sold home yourself for a closer look, if necessary. Ask the agent to produce a copy of the multi-list information, if not already provided to you, not just the computer comparison read out. Any personalized remarks on the MLS *information card* may reveal why these homes sold for less. There should be an information box located on the *information card* where agents write in personal comments, remarks or added features.

Wily agents can easily produce several *comparable* properties to prove lower values if they need to. Uninformed owners may rely on this information and be easily duped into believing their home's market value is lower than what they anticipated. Better yet, if you have any questions, talk to the new owner of a home that sold for less. Find out why the home sold for less. You must learn to be an informed seller. This is your money we're talking about, your bottom line.

Sounds overwhelming? It needn't be. Think one thing through at a time. Begin with your fair market value, then location, then condition, include improvements, then make adjustments for the current market then verify. Be careful not to overdo it.

WHERE AND HOW TO GET THE INFORMATION

I know what your thinking. I'm suggesting using agents to help you establish the fair market value of your home knowing full well you have no intention of listing your home with them. That is correct. That is your right. Offering the seller of a property a free CMA, with no obligation to list, is a standard service offered by real estate agents everywhere. No one in the business charges the owner for this service and no one expects homeowners to list with them because of a free market analysis. You should not feel obligated. The agents will do their very best to persuade you to list with them but the final decision is yours.

THE BY OWNER CUSTOMER (YOU)

Let's assume that after meeting several real estate agents you like one of them and later decide to work with that agent to help you find a home while your home is for sale or after you sell your home by-owner. Once you sell your home you become a qualified prospect. Do you think agents will turn you away as a potential buyer because you didn't list with them? Money is money and agents live off commission. They will seize the opportunity to help and chances are you will be upgrading to a better home in your next purchase (which equates to a hefty commission). They won't turn you away. I guarantee it. It may seem like a contradiction but when you think this through you will see it is your right to change your mind, sell by-owner, and purchase a new home with the help of an agent, if you choose to do that.

AGENT CO-OPERATION

Let's assume for a moment that a month has gone by and you haven't had many buyers through your home. One of the agents contacts you for permission to show your home to a prospect who may be interested. The agent may have a buyer suitable for your home. Are you, at that moment going to turn away a potential sale? I doubt it. You may consider allowing the agent to show your home, and since your home is not a listed property, you are free to negotiate a lower commission. Make sure there is no 'listing contract', not even the so called 24 hour listing contract, between you and the agent other than a signed agreement that stipulates once they show your home, and if they sell it, you will pay a fee that has been agreed upon beforehand, between you and the agent. This is something you must agree to *before* they bring a prospect through your home.

NEGOTIATING THE CO-OP COMMISSION

Commissions are always negotiable. Nothing is carved in stone when it comes to commission. Don't let anyone *bamboozle* you into thinking otherwise. Many agents will play the "our office charges a flat 6% or 7% commission" game. Your response could be, "but you've done nothing to promote our home and at zero expense. How then can you justify charging us a high commission?"

41

Be careful not to fall into the commission trap; the trap that speaks of what is the *norm*. There is no norm. There is no standard percentage or flat rate fee. The commission is whatever the two of you agree on. You may consider offering a flat 2% or 3% of the sales price, certainly no more than this. Be reasonable but play it smart.

What is also important to know is if the agent is on a 100% commission plan with their broker. This plan allows agents the flexibility to charge whatever fee they deem necessary to make a deal work. The days are long gone when an agent can demand a higher commission rate for showing a home once and writing an offer. The 100% commission plan agent has more flexibility than a traditional office agent with respect to making decisions without conferring with the broker. The reason I point this out for you now is for you to see that you have options if you chose to deal with an agent.

I remember times when I cut my commission just to make a deal work. Some agents may pretend to play hard ball but when they realize the owner is serious and is willing to bend to make the sale but only if the agent is willing to bend on commission then the ball falls in the agent's court.

I remember one negotiation where the buyer and seller were only $2,000 apart. Both had compromised as far as they were willing to go. The transaction was at a stalemate. The co-op agent and myself conferred with our broker (who has the final say on lowering commission in a traditional office) and we each gave up $1,000 of our commission. Everyone was content and happy at making the deal. The reason I'll never forget that sale is because it was the first time I gave up some commission to assist a seller in making a sale.

Don't ever think an agent is going to stay firm at a certain commission when you are selling by-owner. Once you grant an agent permission to show your home and agree to pay a fee upon the acceptance of the price set forth in the agreement, and the agent brings in a lower offer, that can change everything, including the amount you will have to pay in commission if the agreement is worded in such a way that allows the commission to change accordingly.

Also be careful with the wording in the agreement. If the language locks you into paying a set commission even when your home sells at a lower asking price then you may consider altering the language before signing the agreement allowing for a renegotiation of the commission.

AGENT ASSISTANCE

Let us also assume you liked one of the agents you spoke to earlier and the agent offered you some assistance while you are selling your home by-owner. Some agents are known to give the by-owner seller documents, such as a disclosure statement or a sales contract. They may even offer to assist you with the drafting of the sales contract once you have a buyer. Agents who are willing to help you through your by-owner experience realize that you may be a buyer one day. Their hope is that you will remain faithful and work with them during your own future buying experience. Agents who are willing to help you through such situations are the types of agents I sincerely hope you meet during your initial contacts.

Use the services of a real estate agent when necessary. Obtain their professional opinions on market value, study the computer print outs and multi-list information cards of like kind homes and get them to help you set your asking price. If need be, interview several agents. Never fall for the line "I'm a top listing agent" or "I sell five million a year." These may be half-truths and for the most part gross exaggerations. Top listing agents are just that, listers of homes. They list em and leave em. It's all a numbers game to them. If they list 100 homes a year 40 homes may actually sell with the help of the multiple listing service, certainly not through their efforts. Agents who both list homes and work with buyers are your best bet. These are agents who will be the most helpful and who are knowledgeable when it comes to working with prospects (which you will be one day).

OPINIONS DO COUNT

Outside opinions are very *helpful* and also crucial to your success when selling your home by-owner. There is nothing more sad than having an overpriced home that requires new paint, new carpets, new countertops, new this and new that. **You should NOT rely on your judgment alone, or those close to you, when establishing the value of your home or judging your home's condition.**

If you will, indulge me for a moment while I tell you a true story. I knew a couple who lived in a quaint, rural community about 45 minutes from a major metropolitan city. Their home was a stately Victorian in pretty good condition. The lot was large and faced a picturesque pond, which was conducive to fishing and recreation. The owners had converted a huge, detached garage into a commercial building suitable for home business applications. The walk out basement beneath the garage was also converted into a two bedroom rental unit and had a lovely view of the water. This was not your average run-of-the-mill home or property. Although far from a major city the home was in a class by itself and it was therefore very difficult to establish a fair market value. Because of its location, age, and uniqueness this type of property would only appeal to a select group of buyers.

The owners ran a test ad six months prior to the time they really planned to sell their home and priced it for $99,900, which brought several buyers but no takers. When I discovered they were selling their home below market value I encouraged them to list it for $150,000. They balked and said it was way too high. After a few more months had passed they decided to list their home with a *friend* in the real estate business, but never placed a 'for sale' sign in the ground. Strangely, their friend had no idea of the market value of the home so the owners set the price at $135,900, a compromise between the $150,000 I suggested and their previous asking price of $99,900.

Within several days of its being listed a neighbor close by discovered the home was for sale and immediately (which is another story) purchased the home through a local realty agency. Not knowing the true value of their home the owners accepted an offer of $124,000. When the appraisal came back it was $13,000 higher than the offer they had accepted and signed. Did they feel stupid? You bet! They felt they cheated themselves out of thirteen grand. The happy new owners closed the deal and the couple now will never forget to seek outside advice. The moral to this story is if you don't know, ask, or hire someone who does know.

Overpricing your home is as bad as underpricing it. If necessary, be prepared to come down in price. Everything is negotiable and should be. Don't make the mistake of putting an asking price on your home that will be your final selling price.

Another example: several years ago I sold a new "spec" home to a couple on a contingency (not a good thing to do) who wanted to sell their own home first. After hours of discussion I finally convinced them to list their home with a broker friend of mine. After many showings a prospect finally made them an offer, which they countered with their full asking price. Their reason for insisting on full price was they felt that since they were paying me full price for their new home they couldn't see coming down in price for their existing home (as if one thing had to do with the other). NEVER, NEVER penalize a buyer or jeopardize the sale of your existing home by demanding full price just because you think you might not have gotten the deal you wanted for a new home that you purchased. One negotiation has nothing to do with the other.

Part II

TERMS

Exactly what does *terms* mean? It refers to how the home will be financed, or the nature of the financing options available to pay for the home. This is where you must be very careful.

Many buyers looking to purchase homes will invariably ask, "what are the *'terms'* of the sale?" They may be wondering if you are willing to carry a note, an 'owner-carried mortgage,' or hold "paper," meaning a 'land contract sale,' also referred to as 'an installment sale,' or, are willing to help pay points for an FHA, VA or other government insured loan program.

Assume nothing. *Terms* can mean many different things. The best way to find out what buyers mean by *'terms'* is to simply ask. You may be surprised to learn that they just spoke to a mortgage company or other lender who pre-qualified them under a specific loan program that carries hefty out-of-pocket fees. You may also learn that they don't have all the closing costs, not surprising since some mortgage companies charge outrageous fees. Your buyers may have the required down payment, 5%, 10% or 20%, but lack thousands of dollars in loan fees or "points" needed to close the deal and may be looking to you for assistance. [Section V will cover this type of negotiation and Section VII will explain who is responsible to pay for what costs.]

Terms, as mentioned above, may refer to whether you are willing to *hold paper* on your home, which, depending on the state you live, could mean a *Land Contract* sale, otherwise referred to as an *installment sale*. Land Contracts were devised years ago to allow home and vacant land buyers to purchase directly from owners to avoid banks or loan companies. Under such a contract the buyer arranges with the owner to pay a monthly payment. Title is not transferred to the buyer until the price is paid in full. This type of sale, although questionable to use in a good market, can often benefit both parties when necessary to use.

It is not my intention here to discuss the pros and cons of a Land Contract sale. This subject would take another section to cover thoroughly. If you are ever approached with this question by a buyer ask your attorney or tax preparer since there may be some ramifications or tax benefits to this type of sale when trying to spread out any capital gains. Unlike Michigan, your state may not allow a land contract sale. I will give you one very recent example of why some buyers prefer to use a *Land Contract*.

I was approached by a prospect who expressed interest in one of my ready to move into "spec homes". He claimed he was flying back to Utah in a day or two to negotiate a sale on his cabin in the mountains and would call me once his sale was locked in. He did just that. However, he sold his home in Utah to a buyer with $85,000 down on a two year *Land Contract* term with full payment due at the end of the two years (balloon payment). He asked if I would sell him a $140,000 home with $85,000 down for the same two year term at 8½% interest. When asked why he did not want a bank loan at 8¼% he expressed his dislike of banks and said he would never borrow a dime from them due to a past experience related to his business. His distrust of lenders forced him into a narrow market where he could only purchase a home under a Land Contract.

CREATIVE FINANCING

Terms may also refer to a partial "owner carried" mortgage and note, called a *Purchase Money Mortgage*, because the money (paper equity, no actual exchange of cash) is used to help purchase the home. This *paper equity* works to the benefit of the buyer. In some circles this is referred to as a *second mortgage* if there is already a first mortgage on the property.

The purchase money mortgage will often make the difference between being able to buy a home or not. Let me cite one example to further illustrate this. When I moved to a small rural community many years ago I was fortunate to find a beautiful home, which I rented for a year with an option to buy. After one year I proceeded to buy the home but found that the local banker would lend me only 70% of the purchase price because they felt I had overpaid for the home. I did not have the remaining 30% for the down payment but did have 20% so I asked the owner to *carry* 10% of the price of the home on a *Purchase Money Mortgage* at a specific monthly payment and interest rate. Both payments, the bank loan and the owner carried mortgage and note combined, were close to what I would have paid the bank each month if I could have financed 80% of the house.

This little known secret to financing part of the down payment

47

through the owner of the home is widely used in California and other states where home prices are significantly higher. Although the buyer is actually borrowing money (paper equity–no exchange of cash) from the seller this portion (the paper equity) is considered the buyer's equity since the lender(s) will be giving the buyer 80% loan financing. At closing the seller will then end up with 90% equity in hand, assuming the buyer is putting 10% down in cash and borrowing 10% on a purchase money mortgage from the seller. In this example the seller will carry a note and a small mortgage for the balance (10%).

In the past when interest rates were very high we often used the 'purchase money mortgage.' We called this 'creative financing.' We sort of knew, though we had no idea how long it would take, that rates would eventually drop. The 'owner carried mortgage' is a unique way to assist buyers with a lower monthly payment. Without this, in periods of high interest rates, many would not be able to buy homes. The 'purchase money mortgage' may not be as popular a financing tool today, as it was during periods of high interest rates, but I assure you it pays to know of this creative financing tool in the event someone needs to show more equity to finance a purchase. This creative financing tool may help you one day with buying or selling a home.

It is important to note that the terms of the purchase money mortgage and note are negotiated separately from the price of the home. Also, in order for the seller to feel confident that the buyer has good intentions of paying off the purchase money mortgage in the length of time repayment should be between five to no more than ten years. A seller would probably consider a fifteen-year note or longer if the buyer's down payment was substantial.

This creative financing tool is important to remember. Any specific questions concerning a purchase money mortgage should be addressed to an attorney.

POINTS

Terms may also refer to 'points.' *Points* is a commonly used mortgage phrase that means only one thing, *money*. One point equals 1% of the loan. When a lender tells you the loan costs 2½ points the 2½ represents 2½% of the loan amount. In other words a loan of $100,000 will cost $2,500 or 2½% of the loan. Points may also be used to buy down an interest rate by prepaying a fixed amount of interest on the loan to induce a lender to lower the interest rate when a buyer has difficulty qualifying for the full loan amount. A lower interest rate can lower the buyer's monthly principal and interest payment allowing the buyer to qualify for the loan in cases where a loan approval may be marginal.

Terms may also refer to points paid for a government 'insured' loan like one of many FHA or VA plans (veteran loan). In the *old days* the seller was required to pay points to the mortgage company at closing if the buyer chose to finance the home via FHA or VA. Choice was not an option then. The seller was helpless and at the mercy of *market conditions* on or near the day of closing. Today, buyers, if they qualify, are allowed to pay for or finance points up front or bury them in the loan, along with closing costs, depending on the type of loan program.

Your buyers may ask you for 'terms' since they may need help from you to make the deal work. It would benefit you to have a clear and thorough understanding of what is expected of you before you refuse their request. Looking back, you yourself at one point may have been one of those buyers who sought a seller's financial help to buy a home. For this reason I always remain flexible to price and terms. More often than not something can be worked out so long as both parties are willing to compromise. In Section V I discuss negotiating with your buyers, with reference to paying some of their mortgage expenses. Sometimes it pays to *sweeten* the pie.

WILL THE BUYER OR SELLER SAVE THE COMMISSION?

When interviewed, most people who chose to sell by-owner said the main reason was to save the commission, or that they had a prior negative experience with a real estate agent or realty company. So saving the commission is the number one reason why people sell by-owner. Unlike selling a car by-owner selling your own home is both challenging and rewarding. Some sell their homes by-owner because they prefer to represent themselves and not depend on others. They want to be in control.

Who will save the commission is an age-old question when selling by owner. Picture this, a buyer comes along and decides to purchase a home, which is for sale by-owner. The asking price is $149,900. The buyer offers the owner $140,000 and explains why the lower offer was made. The buyer, thinking the owner would gladly come down in price to $145,000 for a qualified buyer, which is probably true, since comparable homes in the area are selling for around that price, also realizes the owner would be saving 6% or 7% commission, or around $9,000 - $10,000. In the buyer's mind offering a net sale price of $4,000 to $5,000 more than other homes have netted after paying a full commission is more than reasonable.

The owner in turn deducts ½ of a potential 7% commission from the original asking price of $149,900 and makes a counter offer of $145,000, thinking this is reasonable since they "lowered the price." The buyer makes another offer of $142,000, pointing out that the owner is netting $6,000 to $7,000 more than similar properties in the area. The owner doesn't agree and kills the offer by staying firm at $145,000. The buyer, in this example, with the help of a local real estate agent, finds a comparable home six blocks away and successfully negotiates a purchase for $143,000.

What should the owner have done differently to save this sale? For starters, the seller was asking $5,000 more than the estimated high end for the home. Although not necessarily an outrageously high asking price other comparable homes were priced around $147,900. Bathed in greed the owner felt it necessary to set a price higher than the competition, since the owner believed any buyer will most likely try to lower the price, which is normal in any negotiation. Assuming the owner will **never** receive an offer more than fair market value, or about $145,000, the expected commission would be around $9,000 to $10,000 if it were listed property. This means the **net sale price** after commission would be around $135,000 to $136,000.

The homeowner, in this example, decided to sell by-owner to save the entire commission of $10,000, which is not uncommon. The minute you deal with a knowledgeable buyer who understands the significance of the commission savings it is in the seller's best interest to acknowledge this instead of pretending it doesn't exist, that is if you are genuinely interested in working with a particular buyer to sell your home.

It may even be wise to split the commission, if asked, or share some of it with the buyer to show you're willing to give a fair deal. Partnering with a buyer can be a win-win. Unfortunately the "greed factor" often comes in. Once homeowners feel they have a strong buyer for their home they forget their goal, which is to sell the home. Conversely, it may be unrealistic to expect to sell the home for the full $145,000 market value, though entirely possible in a seller's market, depending on the location of the property.

In the hypothetical example above the seller should have considered the buyer's last counter offer of $142,000. This puts the seller only $3,000 under fair market value and a grand total of $7,000 ahead in commission savings.

Although it's a good bargaining tool, buyers seldom consider the sellers commission to negotiate a better price with a by-owner seller. They are not 'commission savvy' and don't understand that the commission can be a serious negotiating tool when purchasing a home. Understanding what your buyer is trying to accomplish is a strong advantage in selling your home by-owner. You should keep an open mind and remember every buyer is different. Because of the gross commission amount you will have much more flexibility selling by-owner than if your home were listed with a real estate broker under any market conditions.

The most important lesson in selling by-owner is to remain flexible and open to negotiation. No one likes to pay full price and no one should be expected to pay full price for a home. You should consider an asking price for your home only slightly higher than you wish to sell it for, leaving room for negotiation. An asking price of $10,000 more than what the market will bring is unreasonable for a $150,000 home. But an asking price of $2,000 to $3,500 more is fair for this price range as is an asking price of $7,000 more for a $250,000 home, which equates to a 2%- 3% over market value asking price.

If a home is in need of cosmetic upgrading or home improvements (i.e. new roof, cement work, siding replacement, furnace replacement) a buyer will usually see this and will try to make a lower offer to reflect the cost of certain improvements. The mistake we sometimes make is setting this adjusted price beforehand, thinking we are helping the buyer. It may be best to price your home the same as comparable homes of the same size and style even though other homes may be in slightly better condition to allow buyers to use their own judgment when making you an offer. Although the show-ability of the home is critical for making a sale it is debatable which repairs or improvements may be necessary to help the home sell faster.

You should know that in some cases by-owner sellers may not be able to save the *entire* commission. Keep this in mind when selling by-owner and you won't be disappointed, and while in many cases you can save all the commission, in other cases you will only save 50% or more of the commission, which is still substantial these days.

PREPARING YOUR HOME TO BE SOLD BY OWNER

Do you remember the expression, *"dress for success?"* Why do you think it is important for people in business to *"look"* like they are successful? First impressions count, whether a person, a home, or merchandise. This is a known fact in advertising and marketing. There is usually only one chance to make an impression.

The most difficult thing for me to do as an agent was to tell owners to clean their home, cut the grass, change or clean the carpet, paint the house, buy a new front door, or hang a beautiful storm door, deodorize the home, tell the kids to pick up their *stuff* and keep a neat and clean bedroom. It isn't easy but it has to be done.

Nothing turns a buyer off more than a dirty, animal smelly, cluttered and musty home. Cleaning and commercial deodorants can do wonders for the home as will new paint colors.

If you have outdated, *color clashing* countertops, you should consider replacing them with something neutral. Laminate type countertops (Formica, Wilsonart, Pionite, etc.) can usually be installed by the homeowner. There are many companies that offer pre-made, custom, cut-to-fit countertops with hundreds of colors to choose from. I don't recommend buying new cabinets or new carpet throughout, new this or new that unless they have deteriorated to the point where they may hurt the sale. To save up front costs you may consider the replacement of these items to be part of the negotiation. Buyers will see these replacement items as out-of-pocket expenses and if they like your home they will make you a fair offer based on the replacement or updating of certain cosmetics. The best advice I can give you is to fix-up and clean-up as much as you can before offering your home for sale. **Your price will depend on it!**

I once listed a home in a hot selling area that had not sold with two previous agents. This equates to 180 days of lost market time. To find an expired listing in this particular neighborhood was rare. To find a home unsold in 180 days was unheard of. They had priced their home slightly below market value, a fact they assumed would facilitate a quicker sale, but it had not. I told the owners to raise the price several thousand dollars to bring it in line with the rest of the market. They were shocked at my suggestion since the home had not sold at the lower price. I told them the reason their home didn't sell was because of the bright orange countertops. They loved their kitchen counters but after I explained what buyers like and don't like they agreed to purchase new countertops, which cost $600 installed (back then). They sold their home within several weeks for $3,000 more than their previous asking price, all because of new countertops.

I recount this to show that certain cosmetic improvements can dramatically improve the overall appearance or *show-ability* of a home. What looks fine to us may be offensive to a prospective buyer. Fixing up your home pays. It doesn't cost. Think of it this way, if you invest in your home, paint, fix, and clean up, and make the place spic and span until it is "buyer ready" and prospects come through the home and pay you compliments, then negotiate to purchase your home, isn't that better than your home sitting on the market and your making excuses to the buyer about why you don't have the time or money to fix, paint, clean or replace certain items? It's much cheaper to make the necessary changes than to offer your buyer a discount on your home. "Oh, Mr. and Mrs. Buyer we'll take off $2,000 if you paint the home, clean the home, clean the carpet when you move in." What a turn off! "Sure! How about $5,000 off?" says the buyer. The better the home shows the better the deal. This is a proven fact.

Clean your home, clean your carpets, paint your walls (if needed), cut the grass, keep after your kids about maintaining a neat and clean bedroom and pick up all the debris scattered around your house before a showing - and oh, one more thing, send the dog outside or downstairs to play so it doesn't jump on your prospect. These simple steps will help you sell your home faster, and for more money.

Be critical. Walk through your home with pen and paper in hand and write down everything that needs some touch up. Then ask a friend to be objective and do the same thing. Then compare the two lists. If you have too much furniture remove some and store it. An uncluttered home appears roomier. Remember, this is only temporary and it will help you sell.

A SELLER'S MARKET VERSES A BUYER'S MARKET

The real estate market may change drastically and without warning. Shortly before you offer your home for sale you should get current data on 'sold' and 'for sale' properties near you (as previously discussed). For example, early in 2000 interest rates rose rapidly. The higher the rates climbed the more the market reacted as people rushed out to buy homes, fearing yet higher rates were around the corner. As summer rolled around home sales slowed down. The Feds' goal was to slow things down a bit. They succeeded in doing just that.

Prior to that the market seemed to be a "seller's market," which abruptly turned into a "buyers market." If you were to place your home for sale in March for $150,000, and it was not sold by July, you would soon be asking $147,900 or lower, or your home would remain on the market longer than you wished.

Simply put, a buyer's market or a seller's market is based on supply and demand. When there is an ample supply of homes for sale and fewer buyers around to purchase this creates a buyer's market. At such a time, buyers are in control of where they will spend their money. They will be out for the best deal they can find: price, terms, condition, location and amenities.

Taking into account all that we have said in this section thus far it is more than fair to say that even in a buyer's market, as a by-owner seller, you are still in the driver's seat. You have much more flexibility in selling your home than sellers whose homes are listed with real estate agencies. For example, you could lower your asking price instead of offering your home at the current market value. You could advertise, "appliances included," or, "seller will pay buyer's closing costs." These and other headlines will attract buyers in any market to your home. When a buyer does make you an offer but needs further incentive, you could easily negotiate with several thousand dollars of expenses you may be willing to pay on their behalf. Think of this in terms of giving up part of your commission savings.

As a by-owner seller you have, in my estimation, more control, more flexibility, and much more negotiating power than others simply because you are in the driver's seat. But you do need to keep abreast of the changing market so your price and terms stay in line with current conditions. Use a good market or a slow market to your advantage and you will sell regardless of market conditions.

GOOD TIMES, BAD TIMES

I believe that since 1985 we have been experiencing a very healthy real estate market. During this growth period there were bad times and good times with high and low peaks. Although these "swings" may not necessarily dictate a long term 'buyer' or 'seller' market it is important to note, should you try and sell your home by owner during a slower market season (unrelated to summer-winter-spring or fall), that it may take longer to sell. You should always allow ample time to accomplish your goal, and that is to sell your home by-owner and save as much of the commission as possible.

Let us hope we never again experience the recession of 1980-1985. If we do then know this: even then homes were selling, maybe not so fast and maybe not as many, but they were selling and I was still very busy selling homes when prices dropped as much as 10%-20%. Before the recession I was selling around eight homes a month. During the recession I sold three, maybe four a month. During a slow period the by-owner market will also slow down. This does not mean it will be impossible to sell a home but it will be more challenging.

Selling a home by-owner is advantageous in both a good market or not so good market, good times or slow times, primarily because the by-owner seller has everything going for them: Internet exposure, expert advice, flexibility of pricing and incentives, more negotiating power and the ability to be in control.

Section III

HOW, WHY, and WHERE you should advertise your home-for-sale.

You will learn how easy it is to advertise and market your home *effectively.* Everything is discussed from brochure creation to media advertising and much more (including an innovative idea no one has yet thought of). I discuss:

- **Where, When and How to Advertise and Market your home for maximum effectiveness.**
- **Placement of your home on a By-Owner Web Site.**
- **Creating effective signs, brochures and ads to market your home.**

Thanks to the Internet successful by-owner sales are on the rise, which means your chances of selling by-owner have increased as well.

INTRODUCTION

If you've made a commitment to sell your home by-owner then you can expect to foot the bill for advertising expenses. The question you may be asking yourself is how much should you budget? That is entirely up to you. It wouldn't be fair for me to suggest a specific dollar amount, or for you to establish a budget in advance of offering your home for sale without knowing how long it will take or what expenses it will entail. You would not be fair to yourself to say "after we spend X amount of dollars, if we haven't sold our home, we will list it and let the agent pay the expenses." After all, it will come out of your pocket either way.

Why? Think of it this way. You put your home up for sale during a peak buying/selling period and you budget $500, not knowing what all it will entail. One month goes by, you spend that amount, then give up.

So you list your home with an agent, sell it three weeks later and pay out $8,000 in commission. Now you're out $8,500 instead of $8,000. Ouch! You may feel good about spending only $500 cash but how good do you feel about losing $8,000?

Did you really give it enough time? Or do you feel that spending your own money was risky and too adventurous?

You may not have to spend $500 a month for advertising but I assure you to keep your home properly exposed to the market you will be spending at least half that amount. One of the problems with setting an expense budget beforehand is unscheduled expenses that may become necessary. You know if you are prepared to spend the necessary dollars for advertising expenses.

In your household, if you already have a budget for bills, food, car and home, the added expense for advertising a home may not be in your budget. A few by-owner folks begin this task only to realize it's costing them hard cash so they quickly bail out and "list" with a real estate agent, thinking they will save money. But they soon realize that the gross commission will come out of their net proceeds at closing and will be far more than what they would have spent on advertising. Sure, it didn't cost you any cash up front to list your home but the fact is it will cost you more cash at the tail end. So think this through.

If you don't plan to give it your best shot, allow ample time to sell, faithfully market and advertise your home, approach selling your home professionally, then all you will have spent is a few dollars for this book and you can go about your business and move on, list the home with someone you believe will sell your home, let them pay the advertising expenses, let them make the $8,000, or more, in commission. Maybe next time, so you say.

WHERE, WHEN AND HOW TO
ADVERTISE AND MARKET YOUR HOME

As we've already learned, selling a home depends on timing. To bring about the timing one must expose the home to the public by every means possible. One never knows where a potential buyer will come from, whether from the local area or out of state. To expose your home to the public means having a consistent marketing plan throughout the selling period.

Advertising pays, it doesn't cost. Even if your home is listed with an agency, the average real estate office will not advertise your home every week. You won't see it on the cable network or the real estate channel and you may not see it in a home magazine. Why, because agencies have hundreds of properties to sell, not one. They can't possibly afford to advertise every home. They select specific homes with prices and features that will bring in calls to their office in the hope their agents will convert those calls into sales of similar homes best suited to their clients.

Since you have only one home to sell, your marketing efforts will be concentrated on your home. I believe, if you consistently expose your home to the public, you will get as good a response as a real estate office listed home. The rest is up to you.

If you believe that your home will sell within a certain time frame because of its price, condition and location, then your expenses may be relatively small. By following some simple guidelines for marketing your home you will be able to stretch out your advertising dollars. Don't dwell on spent advertising dollars. Look forward to your goal and be positive. You need to make a plan and stick to it. The only thing that will interfere with marketing your home properly is sitting right between your ears. If after a reasonable attempt you've had zero calls, zero showings, zero interest then it's obvious that you need outside assistance, or, that maybe, your price, condition and location may be playing a key factor. One more thing, do not expect to sell overnight or too quickly. Some homes sell quickly and others do not. It will happen when it's supposed to happen.

One example of how unpredictable selling a home can be sometimes, despite the best marketing plans, is something that happened to me in March, 2000. Since business was pretty good in 1999 I expected 2000 to boom. I invested several thousand dollars in TV commercials, weekly newspaper ads (two of them), monthly home magazine ads and a daily Cable TV commercial. All this equates to many advertising dollars. Traffic in March and April was fantastic, but unbelievably, no sales. I had three beautiful spec homes ready for purchase but no takers. I didn't sell any vacant lots in the development either. A few months later, out of the blue, all three spec homes sold including two vacant lots, and several prospects came forward and talked about building later that year. Unexpected? You betcha.

You never know when it will happen but I assure you, it will. All you can do is plant the seeds. They will grow if you spread em around. As long as you are persistent and your home is exposed to the public, traffic will come and a buyer will show up at your door. That is inevitable. Be patient. Think positive.

BROCHURES (FACT SHEETS)

Hanging fliers on bulletin boards at work, at the local supermarket and passing them out randomly is good but not enough. Designing a flyer or a brochure is a must. Once these documents are saved on your computer you can easily modify them when necessary. If you need to know what information to put in a flier look for a brochure box hanging on a real estate sign somewhere in your neighborhood and take one. Collect several brochures from different homes or visit a real estate open house some Saturday or Sunday and pick up a flyer or brochure.

Every piece of information about your home should be included in the flyer, including but not limited to, the exact age of the home or the year it was built, annual property taxes broken down for winter and summer, if applicable, gross square footage, energy efficient features, if any, improvements made to the home, if any, such as brand new furnace professionally installed in 1999, finished basement with a wet bar, natural or woodburning fireplace, unfinished, finished or partially finished basement or lower level walk out and closet or storage description is a must. Typically, every amenity, each room with interior dimensions, should be listed in this brochure. Don't forget to show the price, address and style of the home (i.e. 3 BR - 2 1/2 BA two-story Colonial). A small photo would be nice as well. The photo will serve as a reminder for those who may get confused as to which home they visited and found interesting.

The brochure does not have to be elaborate but should be done on a word processor so bulleted items and features stand out. Once you design the brochure, print it on a good quality 28lb or 38lb stock paper, preferably with color or a designer paper. The handout should also mention that a Home Warranty is available including a Seller's Disclosure Statement, if applicable (Home Warranties and Seller's Disclosures will be discussed in forthcoming sections).

I also strongly suggest hiring your children, or neighborhood kids, to go door to door for several blocks in each direction and hand out brochures to all the neighbors. You will be amazed how often people in the immediate area know someone who wants to buy a home in your neighborhood. Make sure they rubber band the flier to the door and not simply drop it in the mailbox. I've sold many homes by using the *neighbor-who-knows-somebody-who-wants-to-buy* theory. I always hire kids to go door-to-door and pass out fliers. It works! This may turn out to be your best source of advertising.

SIGNS AND BROCHURE BOX

The second thing you should do is to place a sign on your front lawn to let the public know your home is now for sale. The hardware store bought 'For Sale By Owner' sign or a homemade sign lacks appeal (see adjacent picture of an actual handmade by-owner sign that looks, well, sort of blah). You are better off going to a sign company where for about $50 they can make a sign that says "Home For Sale By Owner, 777-555-1212". I found many local FSBO services offering a set package including signage, advertising and other services. You should also visit www.sellitbyownerandsave.com to see if we are offering for sale by owner sign and other products

For several reasons, I favor using a brochure box attached to the sign or on a separate lawn stake. I've found over the years that people like to read something about the home before they inquire. The *box* is user friendly and it shows a potential buyer you are willing to describe your home's amenities. The brochure is a great way to explain appointment scheduling, who to contact for a showing, list work and home phone numbers, etc.

Don't be discouraged if after 20 or 30 brochures you haven't received a call from potential buyers. I go through dozens of brochures in a week's time. The main thing to remember here is traffic. If they're taking your brochure from the box it means they drove past your home and found it interesting enough to stop and get the information. Showings will come. Be patient.

A good quality brochure box usually costs around $30.00. You should try our web site to see if we are offering our customers a brochure box.

EXPECT THE UNEXPECTED

Now that you have a sign in front, and a brochure box, you can expect passersby to stop and ask to see your home, perhaps without an appointment. This happens frequently whether your home is listed with an agency or not. You should handle unscheduled showings tactfully, politely reminding them that your sign or brochure does specify "by appointment only." You don't want to lose potential prospects even if they seem rude or put off by the fact that you are unable to show them the home at that moment.

In the event a prospect comes to the door and demands to see your home someone with authority should answer the door and politely, yet firmly, instruct the person to call for an appointment since it is not convenient at the moment. Displaying a sense of urgency is a tactic some buyers and real estate agents may use to gain entry to a for sale by-owner home. You should have a stack of brochures nearby and offer them one, just in case they missed the brochure box, then encourage them to call you for an appointment at their earliest convenience.

Remember this, very few buyers walk into a realty office and demand to see homes immediately. Usually, the agent schedules showings a day ahead giving homeowners ample time to prepare their home for showing. Don't feel that by chasing prospects away you've lost anything. If they are seriously interested they will call, especially after reading your brochure. If they don't call they were tire kickers (time wasters) and you haven't lost a thing. I can't explain why but once your home is officially on the market the public may feel, since you are selling by-owner verses having your home listed with an agency, that they have a right to see your home any time they feel like it. Stick to your agenda. Don't break or bend your rules for anyone. It may seem unwise to turn prospects away but believe me, if they are interested they **will** return.

Since I sell vacant lots and homes from the model home I live in I frequently get off-hour visitors. I used to allow them in to tour the model home but I no longer do. I have yet to see anyone return to purchase a lot or a home who first came by after hours. Yes, I did accommodate them in the beginning but now I no longer offer an unscheduled tour. I give them a brochure and ask them to return during business hours.

NEWSPAPER ADS

Although it is true that nothing sells unless advertised, when it comes to home sales, I've lost faith in newspaper ads. It seems as if a real estate ad gets lost in the volley of other classified ads. Believe it or not many realty companies stopped using newspapers as their main source for advertising. A newspaper is my least favorite media for placing ads. There are several less costly and more productive advertising sources available besides newspapers.

I advertise our development once a week, on Sunday only, in the classified section of a major metropolitan paper. The ad is very small. I do this for only **one reason**. Because my model home is 30 miles from the city in a small rural community and I want people to find my website address. Displaying my web address in the ad is the only reason I continue to run this ad weekly.

I receive, on the average, about twenty visitors a month to my model home. I ask each of them how they found out about our housing community. I attribute one couple a month to a newspaper ad. The *only benefit* I derive by advertising weekly in the newspaper is offering my web address.

When my development first opened, I ran display ads, usually a 4 inch by 3 inch ad, but found they were no more effective than small classified ads at 1/10th the cost. Newspaper ads are expensive.

For best exposure you may consider running one ad in a major newspaper every two weeks but limit the ad to as few words as possible such as: Smith School District; Charming 3BR - 2 1/2 BA Colonial; large lot, amenities galore, excellent condition; asking $149,900; Owner, 555-1212. Include the web address (if you have a web page).

If you live away from a major city (in a rural area, like me) then you may consider alternating between your *local* newspaper and the *big city* paper every other week to get wider coverage. Where I'm located we get a mix of "locals" and "city folks." I randomly advertise in several different local publications to bring in traffic from several directions.

Newspaper ads are hit and miss. An open house ad will draw more attention than the standard classified ad, especially if **OPEN HOUSE** is in big, bold type. You could also consider advertising a 'moving sale' or a 'garage sale' in the newspaper, which will attract dozens of people to your doorstep. Be prepared to sell some of the stuff in your attic or basement (or the extra clutter you've always wanted to get rid of).

HOME MAGAZINES

There are probably several home magazines in your area that you should consider for placing an ad. I've seen by-owner home magazines as well as real estate agency home magazines and newspaper owned and operated home magazines. **Placing an ad in an exclusive by owner publication is highly recommended.**

The 'home magazine' is my favorite way to advertise a home. By comparison, a home magazine ad is larger than a newspaper ad allowing room for more information along with a photo. I believe the more information you give readers the more likely they are to call. This is also a type of pre-qualification since they know where your home is located, the school system, the price, amenities, the square footage, the age of the home, etc. Although you can state these and other statistics in a newspaper ad it is far more costly than a home magazine ad.

PICTURES ARE IMPORTANT

Placement of ads in a home magazine allows you to insert a nice picture or two, depending on the size ad you've purchased. Grab an older picture of your home or take a new one with a digital camera, if possible, showing mowed green grass, if in the summer, with flowers blooming, if in the spring, or if in Autumn, color on the trees with a blue sky for best visible results. People, children, or the family pet in the photo is a winner. Viewers will identify better with human life and pets in the foreground or background. The deadline for submission of home magazine ads is usually several weeks before the next issue release date so you may want to jump-start this and gather all the information on your home and how to place the ad as early as possible. At the end of this section I discuss many of the "key" items to place in your home magazine or newspaper ad.

The cost of a home magazine ad is far less than classified newspaper ads. Keep in mind not to blow your budget entirely on this medium. Find out the market distribution numbers and drop off locations to make sure you're not buying a 'pig in a poke' (a homes magazine that no one will find or read). Once you locate a home magazine you wish to advertise in simply ask them where and how many of their magazines are distributed. Distribution numbers and drop off locations are essential to know when deciding on such magazines. There are some very good by-owner homes magazines around the country.

WEB PAGE ADVERTISING

Thank God for the Internet. We can now disseminate information to thousands of people at a reasonable cost, or for free. There are many on-line services and business centered web sites that offer free web pages for individuals to do with whatever they please, including building their very own personalized web page for whatever purpose. This is **strongly recommended** since you can upload several pictures and describe your home with every possible detail. In all your advertising, brochures and handout material, you should include your web address. If there is any way you could track the hits you will be amazed at how many people will visit your web page and read about your home. All of your advertising combined will not benefit you nearly as much as having a web page or website. It would not surprise me in the least if you sold your home through your very own web presence. You need no extra software, you needn't purchase any additional programs and you may not need any assistance with set up and design.

If you design a web page or website to promote your home I strongly suggest you test the effectiveness of the newspaper ad to draw attention to your web site by running a few minimally worded newspaper classified ads by saying something like this:

> Underpriced at $149,900, 3BR–2½BA colonial in prime area; www.myhouseforsalebyowner.com or 222-555-5555.

This ad is small, will get the word out and will direct people to your web page. Keep it short and simple.

BY-OWNER WEB SITE ADVERTISING

I performed an exhaustive search on the Internet and found many free By-Owner web sites where I was able to post spec homes for sale in my development. I also found many sites that charge $35 to $100 to list your home for sale. Some of these fee based sites had time limits, others were unlimited until the home was sold, yet others charged monthly fees. Only a few I found had proper information boxes and picture-placing assistance. Many were not the quality I would recommend. I judged them on ease of use and their user-friendly interface.

Some sites were specific to certain locations. There is one site I tried for a $50 fee which had limited use for my specific area, yet may be useful in other areas of the country. So you should take note of how effective a site may be for your particular area. Another site I tried was an on-line auction service for "for sale by owner" properties. Auctions are interesting and if they didn't work I suppose on-line auction service companies would be out of business. Real estate auctioning is catching fever and may be the next biggest thing since peanut butter in the not too distant future. Although an on-line auction service may be another viable tool for selling your home there is still a commission involved when selling through these service companies.

A few months before construction was completed I placed two of my spec homes for sale with a free, no-fee, by-owner website. For one thing, I felt the exposure was probably just as good as the fee based service sites. I wasn't willing to pay $30 a month for each home, or a one time fee of $99 for unlimited market time, or a weekly fee to a service that claimed to have several hundred thousand hits a week.

I did receive one call from a prospect, who found one of my spec homes listed on a by-owner site. The buyer claimed to have sold a home by-owner through that same by-owner website service. One can't help wonder why by-owner website placement service companies are popping up like hot dog stands. I believe the reason such sites are growing is they hope to sell banner advertising to banks, lenders, mortgage companies, title insurance companies, insurance companies, home warranty companies, and any other service industry related to the home (and harvest more *hits*). Whether or not any one of these sites in particular is better for you than another depends on their geographical coverage and the information you supply them.

My own observation is this: I noticed many by-owner listed homes lacked a photograph, which is not good. Other by-owner listed homes lacked a phone number for more information or for an appointment to show, which is also not good. Still others had fill-in blanks that were devoid of any information. I think you get my point by now. **IF YOU PLAN TO USE ANY OF THE BY-OWNER LISTING PLACEMENT WEB SITES (free or fee based) BE PREPARED TO COMPLETE FORMS IN THEIR ENTIRETY or DON'T BOTHER.**

Another point is the geographic-specific benefit to some of these sites. Before you spend your time, or invest your money, you should perform a real estate search on these sites. Check to see if any of these sites list homes from your city or immediate area. For example, I found several fee based sites offering national coverage with very few Michigan homes (my area) offered for sale. I also found other sites that offered more homes for sale in Michigan than other states.

Home hunters surfing the web usually skip over these sites and concentrate on other sites where there are more homes to view. Similar to the on-line auction service I experimented with, if a particular site lists very few homes for sale in your area you should consider looking for another web site. If you have a specialty property or resort for sale you may need to perform an exhaustive search to locate an on-line service best suited to your property.

I've also noticed an increase in added services offered through many by-owner web sites designed to pull customers in. For example, some claim you can now establish your home's market value by using their database. This 'database' information may be sketchy. I would be leery of using or relying on their database as a basis for setting a price for my home. Please understand, the information in their data base is data input from prior customers selling their homes. This information may not be reliable or accurate. You should stick to the proven method as described in Section II. Maybe, one day, we will be able to perform a reasonably thorough "sold" search to establish home values using the Internet, but that day hasn't yet arrived. Bank appraisers, fee appraisers, state appraisers, assessors and others in the business of having to establish the value of real estate use comparable data found only in local areas, usually through local sources. I say this to caution you and to alert you to the possibility that these Internet by-owner services probably mean well but you may end up selling yourself short when it comes to the value of your property if you rely on their database.

In closing I am prepared to say this, concerning the national by owner web site services. I feel the larger web sites who offer national coverage are in it strictly for the money; your money and advertising dollars from their partners. I don't believe for one minute a buyer will suddenly appear out of nowhere as a result of their huge inventory of homes. I also don't believe the information they offer may be a true representation of sold properties. It stands to reason if they currently have 500,000 by owner listings that some will sell yet they brag about homes selling through their service as if they had something to do about it first hand.

I have more faith in the local, geographic specific or state specific by owner web site service companies than I do the larger national ones. I believe if folks from Michigan are looking to make a purchase in Michigan then they will seek out Michigan specific web sites. I also believe that out of state buyers looking to purchase a home in Michigan will do likewise. Some of the services I have seen being offered through a state specific web site service is unbeatable and for a price that is very affordable.

ADVERTISING BULLETS

What to say, what not to say, in your ads and brochures; that is the question.

Here is the answer:

- **Price is a must.** People want to know what you are asking for
  your home. They do not appreciate wasting time or money on
  needless phone calls or visits to a property only to find the price
  you are asking is $50,000 more than they can afford. I have never
  agreed with the adage that says "ads bring in calls" when you
  leave out the price. Advertising the price brings in more qualified
  calls. These are buyers who are comfortable with that price range
  or they wouldn't be calling. Once you've established your value
  round off the asking price to the nearest $500 or $900, meaning
  $149,900 instead of $150,000, or $144,500 instead of $144,700,
  etc. I've seen ridiculous asking prices, such as $102,750. What's
  the difference? They may as well ask $102,900.

- **Location is critical.** There is no point in not telling your prospects where your home is approximately located. Except in
  your brochure I would not show an address or street name in
  any ads, unless of course you plan to advertise an *open house*.
  City name (east, west, north or south), suburb name, community name or township name may help sell your home. A specific *named* neighborhood is important to advertise. For example "Indian Village," in Detroit, Michigan, which is syn-
  onymous with architecturally well designed and built homes,
  circa 1920, may be an attraction for potential buyers. These
  homes, embellished with natural oak trim, winding staircases,
  stained glass, sun rooms, butlers quarters, etc., can be a very
  big draw for a large circle of buyers looking to purchase a
  home in this particular neighborhood.

  Accessibility or distance to a local freeway is an added benefit
  for commuters to know. I consistently advertise that our housing
  community is 1¼ miles to the Interstate and 25 minutes to down-
  town. It doesn't hurt to advertise the actual distance, in terms of
  minutes, it takes to drive to a major city. If you are adjacent to or
  near a freeway the noise factor may discourage some lookers. In

your advertising they don't need to know the freeway is in your back-yard, just "convenient access" is sufficient. Find key points to your home which would compensate for the fact that a major artery is right behind you or in front, like *privacy* (meaning no neighbor behind you). If you live on a busy street you might say "excellent location." To you it is excellent since in the winter your road is plowed first or public transportation is close-by. If your home is convenient to shopping, a transportation system, walking distance to churches or schools, let your buyer know this.

- **School system** is optional, unless you positively know your school system is a major draw or selling point, then it becomes *essential*. Certain school systems sell homes. Once word gets out about a particular school system it seems as if buyers look for homes strictly in that district. It may be an important asset to advertise. The buying public may see this as a *treasure to be had*. I've seen many great ads start out by advertising the school system, then the home, then the price and phone number. Take advantage of this buyer-acknowledged benefit and wave the school system out front.

- **Environmental amenities** such as nature walking paths, trees, parks, lake access, water frontage, view of a creek, river, ocean, and anything to do with natural scenery is important. In the late 70's I sold new custom homes adjacent to a famous country club. Once potential prospects discovered this gem adjacent to a famous country club sales were easy. Everyone wanted to build a home behind the 18th hole.

"Access to" is also an important feature not to be overlooked. For example, in some housing or condominium communities there may be water frontage, lakes, rivers, community pools, clubhouses, exercise equipment and numerous other amenities that should not be overlooked. In a recent visit to California I heard of a housing community where mini-railroad tracks were installed by the developer and a real train whistles around the property on a timed schedule. Do not minimize or overlook any amenity, no matter how trivial it may seem to you.

I advertise *"wildlife abounds"* in our community. We have people living here who have documented numerous *forest* animals (no bears) and rare birds. Nature lovers seek out these types of communities. A wooded/treed lot or acreage is also a nice feature to advertise.

WHAT IF MY HOME NEEDS TLC?

If your home is in disrepair, or your home needs some major remodeling you could overcome this in an ad by saying something like this: "Handyman Special; "Home Needs TLC"; "Price Reflects Need for Updating;" "Wanted, Buyer Willing to Make Repairs," etc. You will be amazed at the number of buyers who respond to this type of ad. They are usually willing to take on the work as a project to save a few bucks. These buyers know they will initially invest thousands of dollars in fix-up costs yet they also realize the price of the home will be lower and probably in line with their budget and qualifications. In some cases homes advertised as needing TLC will sell quicker than comparable homes that are priced thousands of dollars higher. It may be in the buyers' best interest to cosmetically modify the home to their own liking while saving a pile of money.

If there is a "fire sale," meaning you need to sell fast and there is little time to lose on the market you could advertise by saying: "Must Sell Fast;" "Super Deal for Ready-Willing & Able Buyer;" "Divorce Forces Sale;" "Relocation Forces Sale." These types of captions will draw more buyers to your home quicker than any other headline for the simple reason prospects feel they may be getting a better deal.

You can never say enough about your home and for this reason I encourage a web page or website specifically designed to sell your home by-owner. You will not regret it.

Section IV

HOW to deal with real estate agents.

This section deals with HOW to get aggressive agents to back off and, conversely, HOW to negotiate a commission with an agent in the event you allow one to bring a legitimate prospect through your home as a co-op venture *(see Glossary)*. I'll explain HOW and WHEN it may benefit you to work with an agent on a limited basis. There are situations where it won't cost you a dime to deal with an agent. I reveal this well hidden secret.

Some agents may hound you (since you are selling by owner) and try to convince you to list your home with them for numerous reasons by using "market hype" or "fear tactics." I want you to be aware of the hype they use and to recognize their pitch when it comes your way. Agents make their living off commission; no sales, no commissions. Some agents tend to exaggerate. A few can be greedy, pushy and quite persuasive. I will illustrate this further.

INTRODUCTION

Never in all my years in the real estate business did I find it necessary to deceive or mislead homeowners for any reason in an attempt to list their home with me. The fact is, in a traditional real estate office, there are days and evenings set aside to cold call "by owner" advertisers, a practice I refused to participate in. The agent's task is to bombard you, bug you daily, wear you down and drive you crazy until you list your home. Their goal is to make you believe "agents are the only ones" who can sell your home. They can be persuasive, highly energized, loquacious individuals who have attended countless seminars and who may have a *delicious* canned speech prepared just for you. They may even show you a computer print out (which is a cheap trick) of what listed homes "like yours" have sold for, thinking perhaps you are clueless, in an effort to prove it is better to list with them than to sell "by owner." Their motives may seem pure but their methods, at times, are deplorable. In short they can and will test your patience. Why? Because you are selling by-owner! And for some unexplained reason they view this as a threat.

The only way I know to get aggressive agents off your back is to tell them several things: First, you can tell them you have a relative in the business who is helping you and who plans to list your home if you don't sell by-owner, or better yet, tell them your son or daughter is an agent. They will ask for their name or which office they work in. You do not have to reveal any information.

Secondly, you can tell them that you have already selected a real estate professional working with XYZ Company in the event you decide to list your home (one of the people who performed your market analysis perhaps). Again, you do not have to reveal any specific information.

Thirdly, you can hang up on them like you would any telemarketer. This step is rude yet sends a clear message.

Many realty offices today use the Bresser's reference book, where they can cross reference any published phone number which can locate an address within minutes. BE PREPARED FOR UNSCHEDULED VISITS BY SOME OF THESE 'HARD WORKING' PEOPLE. And look out if they work in teams. Two is tougher than one.

When and if someone comes to your door to ask for a showing and if you suspect they are in real estate, based on their dress or the car they are driving, ask them outright. If they identify themselves as being a licensed real estate agent you are free to deny them access to your home. If on the other hand they try to convince you that they have a prospect looking for a home in your neighborhood you may want to ask why they don't show the listed home down the street, if there is one for sale. They may say that they have buyers who are looking for a home "just like yours" (now isn't that convenient). Once you let them into your home you will be faced with the same situation as being involved in a timeshare pitch - no escape.

I've known agents who work as a team and pose as a "couple" just to see a by-owner home or they find another couple to pose as a prospect to impress a by-owner seller into thinking they may have a *hot buyer*. I've known agents who lie to owners and swear they have a qualified buyer ready, willing and able to buy their home, if they could only have the listing. Just like the movie, Jerry McGuire, you should shout "SHOW ME THE MONEY" or I'LL SHOW YOU THE DOOR.

If I've painted a picture all real estate people operate this way then I haven't done my profession justice. There are many honest, sincere, professional, caring, and trustworthy agents worthy of dealing with. Should you come across such agents they will be worth their weight in gold; for a mountain of knowledge stands before you; a library of information at your fingertips, all for the asking. Good luck and learn to rely on your own instincts.

NEGOTIATING THE COMMISSION WITH A REAL ESTATE AGENT

Sitting in a model home and selling homes in a new home development is just as challenging as selling a home by owner. There is no difference. I deal with all kinds of prospects as well as real estate agents looking to make an easy buck. I get an occasional call from agents who make a feeble attempt to list or show one of my new homes. I won't list any of them, period. When I give them permission to show a home they immediately discuss commission. They claim their office fee is 6%; sometimes I'm quoted 7%. I politely tell them there is "no room" in our asking price to pay that kind of fee since I don't increase the price of our new homes to accommodate a commission. I usually tell them to look to the buyer to pay their commission. By the time we're done talking we may have agreed on 3%, or less, with an adjustment in the price to accommodate their fee. Once in a while I'll get someone down to 1½ or 2%.

I look at the **big picture** this way: I view this as *"time is money."* If I have to pay a small commission and can sell a home quicker then so be it. In the long run I will pay out less in advertising costs, lower interest to the bank, fewer utility bills and other incidentals that eat away at the bottom line. Except for one recent experience no agent has ever come through my door with a legitimate buyer ready, willing and able to purchase. Most have been fast talkers looking for a listing, hoping to make a quick, easy buck.

One day, I had a visit from a real estate agent only minutes past closing time. He was far from his normal market territory. He lived and worked an hour and a half drive away. It turned out he was related to the buyers and decided to help them into their next home, and presented himself as their agent (buyer's agent) only after he was asked. It appeared he was legitimately under contract with the buyers to represent them in the transaction. This meant he was looking out for their best interest.

After previewing my spec homes his buyers fell in love with one. The agent approached me that same evening to discuss price and terms. At first he wanted to be paid an enormous commission, which I flatly refused. After speaking to his broker he then agreed to 3%. During the final negotiations we agreed to split the 3%. Since I was asking $139,900 for the home I added another $2,100 to the price and agreed to pay a *fixed dollar amount* commission of $4,200, not 3% of the sale price, which only cost me 1-1/2% or $2,100, an amount I would have gladly come down to for any qualified buyer.

The fixed 'dollar amount commission' is a good idea to lock into instead of the fluctuating percentage, especially if there is a counter offer involved. Once you agree in writing to a percentage commission of the sale price and adjust the price upward for other buyer compensations (as you will learn in subsequent sections) you will actually be paying more money in commission than originally intended.

The purpose of this example is to illustrate that *everything is negotiable*. If you have to deal with agents and they seem to have a legitimate buyer remember this story if only to illustrate that nothing is carved in stone when it comes to commissions. There are situations when the commission may be paid by the buyer, as in this example, and there are situations where the commission won't cost you a dime.

AGENT DECEPTIONS

Some agents can be devious. They may dissemble, deceive and try to convince you that they have a buyer in their *pocket* for a home "like yours" and if you want to sell your home they can get your asking price from their buyer but you will have to pay a commission. They use this line quite often so try not to forget it.

If an agent does bring a legitimate buyer to see your home and calls on you to arrange negotiations, you can give the agent several options. Tell the agent that one half the normal commission, or no more than 3% of the sale price is acceptable so long as the buyer offers the minimum acceptable price. If the agent balks let the agent know you wish to be treated as if you were the listing agent, therefore keeping your half of the commission (hypothetically speaking). This is legitimately done in any co-op sale through two brokerage firms.

If the agent throws all the "legal" stuff your way about your not being qualified to close the deal, or handle the title search, etc. etc. and more commission is needed, then be prepared to give the agent the name of the title insurance company who will handle your title insurance policy and closing. This will not only impress the agent that you've done your homework but will end the conversation as well. For your information real estate agents neither "process a sale" or a loan nor do they "close the deal." **They simply *arrange things* as easily as I will teach you to do in forthcoming sections.**

If you resort to dealing with a real estate agent and agree to pay a commission, and the agent drafts and presents you with a sales contract (purchase offer, purchase agreement, offer to purchase), and is acting as a buyer's agent, (which the agent must present to you in writing if that is the case) then you may need the services of a real estate attorney if you are unfamiliar with, don't quite understand, or have reservations about, signing the sales contract. **HIRE A PROFESSIONAL AT THIS POINT** to look over the agreement before signing it if you are uncertain what to do. There may be language, terms or clauses you may not be familiar with or that may seem confusing to you. These can cause problems later on in the transaction should the buyer decide to back out, legitimately or not, and you make an attempt to claim the buyer's good faith deposit. You should **not rely** on the agent to look after your best interests. Remember, the agent is not working for you. You should also not rely on 'explanations' given, even if the agent seems to mean well. The agent is working strictly for the buyer. If you are confused by any of the language in the contract **hire a professional** to interpret the "language" and to explain each and every legal clause before signing.

AGENCY DISCLOSURE & TACTICS

Many states today have legislation governing agency disclosure. More often than not agents who show homes to a buyer are usually regarded as "buyer's agents," meaning they have entered into an agreement with the buyer that they will represent the buyer in a transaction, not the seller. Should the agent tell you that he could also represent you this can later be construed as "dual agency." The agent can be in serious trouble if this dual agency has not been acknowledged and agreed to in writing by both buyer and seller. **This is a very serious matter and should not be treated lightly.**

When presenting an offer to a seller it was generally my goal to persuade the seller to accept the offer without changes or counter offers. I would argue that the buyer's offer was a good one (if in fact it was a good offer) and that the buyer was well qualified and there should be no problem making the deal work. Often, when the offer was lower by several thousand dollars, sellers always appeared disgruntled. It is the job of the agent to present the offer in such a way that the seller understands the circumstances surrounding the buyer's offer and what could happen if the seller decides to counter the buyer's offer. I often did my best to convince the seller to take the deal "as is." This wasn't done to *shortchange* the seller. As agents, we understood the seller's reluctance to accept a lower offer. We merely applied a common sense argument we believed would assist the seller in making a decision to accept the buyer's offer. Because we were zealous in our efforts to "assist" it could have easily been construed that we were working for the buyer, when in fact we were working for the seller. Those were the days before "agency disclosure."

Agents today have learned to use several persuasive tactics. Should you vacillate countering an offer presented by a buyer's agent the agent may imply you are, in essence, *buying back your home*, meaning you are *killing* the buyer's offer thereby having no offer on the table at all because, by virtue of the counter offer, you have literally "bought back your own home." Be careful not to fall for this rhetoric or other verbal games.

There is nothing wrong with a well thought out counteroffer, or no counteroffer. Your decision to counter an offer presented by a buyer or through a buyer's agent should be based on solid reasons such as the offer price in relation to market value or other pertinent terms.

When and if you are faced with agents who are "presenting" an offer on behalf of a buyer remember one important thing: you do not have to accept the offer right away, despite any hype they may feed you, and you're not going to lose the deal if you don't. There may already be a provision in the sales agreement allowing the seller 24 to 72 hours to review and accept the buyer's offer and during that time the buyer cannot withdraw the offer, if the language in the contract prevents them from doing so.

You should also keep in mind there are circumstances that arise in a transaction that may warrant accepting a "lower offer" (lower meaning 2%-5% below your asking price). These circumstances may be directly related to your location, the condition of the home, the original asking price compared to other comparable homes in the surrounding area and the length of time your home has been on the market.

FOCUS ON THE OFFER

Once you look at the offer price and focus on your asking price and see that the two are drastically far apart you may arbitrarily kill the deal, when in reality you should have considered either countering the offer or accepting the offer, especially if the offer price is right on or close to your market value. I say this to alert you to the possibility that you may be focusing too much on your asking price rather than focusing on the true market value of your home. It's important to take all things into consideration when making a decision to accept, counter, or refuse a buyer's offer. I always throw caution to the wind when considering an offer. I look at all aspects of the sale and I seldom, if ever, focus on my asking price.

GREED

I have a great saying, "Greed will get ya." We all experience some level of greed at some point in a buying or selling experience. And the only time greed comes into play is when you have a buyer who expresses an interest in your home and you think your home is the only home the buyer is willing to negotiate on. Until then you may have verbalized your desire to sell and you were thinking when a fair offer comes along you'll accept it. This paradox of wanting an offer so badly you'll take it when offered, then when you receive it and want more money you're willing to risk a sale, has lost many sales for by-owner sellers who easily lose sight of their primary goal. Don't make the mistake of looking a gift horse in the mouth. It is much wiser to think through your reaction to an offer be-fore considering a counteroffer and jeop- ardizing the sale. Think before you speak when it comes to negotiations or you may find your home still for sale long after others in the neigh- borhood have been sold and their own- ers have moved away.

Section V

HOW to deal with prospects, set appointments and show your own home.

I cover, in great detail, the *do's* and *don't's* and explain:

- **HOW to determine if a prospective buyer is *qualified* and *sincere* and not just a window shopper.**
- **HOW to handle appointments.**
- **HOW to show a prospective buyer through your home and suggest WHAT to say and what not to say. On occasion we find ourselves saying too much and talking ourselves out of a sale.**
- **HOW to negotiate with your buyer: More tips and suggestions for a successful sale.**

Part I

UNDERSTANDING YOUR BUYER

Buyers, looky-loos *(see Glossary),* prospects, dreamers (people who love to look at homes well above their means), and potential buyers, will contact you in various ways. Understanding them, their motives, and what they are after will be important in transforming a "showing to a closing."

In my many years of experience dealing with home buyers I have learned that many have a tendency to withhold certain information. This may concern the equity or cash reserve they plan to work with for a down payment, or the gross amount they can swing for a loan, their ability to borrow money or how they really feel about your home. One minute they'll say how much they love your home and it's everything they've dreamed about and in the next breath they rationalize why they shouldn't be buying it. This and other contradictory behavior makes selling a home a continuing challenge.

I am especially fascinated by the variety of fabricated *stories* people will tell. For instance, they may claim when making an offer, and after being faced with a counteroffer, that if they borrow more money they won't qualify for the loan, thus they can't buy the house, thereby justifying their original lower offer. In other words, "Mr. and Mrs. Homeowner, if you want to sell me your home you must come down to my price since if I go any higher I won't *qualify* to buy your home." Too bad!

Lesson number one: Try not to fall for what appears to be a fictitious story. You and I should not be concerned with where the money for their down payment comes from, so long as it is in greenbacks. It matters little if Uncle Harry or Mom and Dad plan to lend them part or all of the money for the down payment so long as their lender gives them a loan approval. It does not interest me to know, nor should it affect my decision, that the buyers have reached their maximum loan amount, and use that to try to persuade me to come down another $5,000 so they can qualify for the loan. The question should be, if they want the home bad enough, isn't it possible for them to find the extra $3,000-$5,000 needed to clinch the deal (perhaps from Uncle Harry)? Why should I be penalized?

I'm certain if they look long and hard they will find money somewhere, like from some sort of 401K-plan or investment fund which for the time they would rather not touch or disclose. If you've already given the buyers a good deal, why should you give up several thousand dollars more in equity to help them purchase your home just because they claim they are on the wire?

They may even produce a letter from a bank showing they are approved for a specific mortgage amount. It is good that they have been pre-qualified. The pre-qualification letter may be perfectly legitimate, however it is **no indication** they won't qualify for a slightly higher mortgage.

Let me give you an example of something you may come across. The buyers agree to a written sales agreement with you and tell you they have been pre-approved at a local bank. They show you a letter to validate this. They tell you the loan amount of $125,000 is the most the bank will give, and, therefore, along with a $15,000 down payment, they cannot offer more than $140,000. You were asking $149,900 and were willing to take $145,000 from a qualified buyer. What should you do? The frustration of dealing with this dilemma can be overcome easily.

Some buyers will exaggerate to justify their actions. Of course, this does not apply to all buyers. Many are straight forward, sincere, forthright and perfectly honest concerning their qualifications, debts, credit history, cash reserves, etc. On the other hand, some will withhold information in order not to disclose certain important facts that may negatively affect their chances of obtaining credit.

One example will suffice. I sold one of my spec homes for $135,000 in the fall of '99 to a very nice couple who had recently moved to Michigan. They were both professionally employed. They previewed the home several times before making the offer at full price. At the time they disclosed that they had "a few credit problems" such as unpaid doctor bills or other incidentals. I assured them if that was the only problem then it shouldn't be a hindrance to getting a loan.

I suggested they try our local bank to start a loan application. To my surprise the bank declined their loan and my banker wouldn't disclose the nature of their credit report to me. I assumed their credit was bad so I sent them to a "C" paper lender, (lenders who provide loans at higher rates to people whose credit is less than favorable). After inquiring why they didn't qualify for the first loan the husband finally disclosed that he was in default on a student loan, which resulted in his being given a poor credit rating. He had hoped the information had gotten lost in the system, but it didn't. The irony is that while the student loan helped him earn a professional degree in a field where he makes $75,000 per year (so he claimed), because of that student loan, which he has defaulted on, he now faces the likelihood that he will not be able to buy a house for years to come because of his poor credit. Amazing!

This same couple offered another convoluted story about their money being "tied up" with a relative whom they were waiting for to liquidate their investments. Without this, they said, they couldn't get their hands on any cash, not even for the good faith deposit (which sounded questionable). Without these monies they said they were penniless. Another fabrication I'm sure.

The contract I drafted stipulated that the deposit was to be paid within two weeks of signing the contract. I allowed a two week time frame to give them ample opportunity to liquidate the 'investment' they claimed they had. I never received a response from them. From the start they were never specific about how much down payment they planned to make or the amount of the loan they were hoping to obtain. This information is important to know for filling out the Sales Contract. When I didn't receive their deposit on the due date, as stipulated in the contract, I killed the deal. I never heard from them again. I put the home back on the market and sold it to a qualified couple who provided full and honest disclosure of their financial and credit history.

Having dealt with hundreds of home buyers I learned it is important to develop a healthy attitude when dealing with customers. I take each case individually and I take them at face value. I don't assume they're lying or withholding information from me. On the other hand, I don't put stock in everything they say either. When they visit my model home and tell me they're interested in buying I smile and wait to see if they return.

LOOK OUT FOR THE THIEF

Buyers are all different in terms of what they know and expect. What interests me most when negotiating with buyers is whether they are sincerely interested in buying a home at a fair price or if they are out to try to "*steal*" one of my homes. The person who is genuinely interested in purchasing a home is one who is more apt to make a fair offer rather than the person who is making an attempt to purchase the home at a ridiculously low offer. I have sold numerous 'spec homes' at full price to buyers who recognize value, compared to buyers who feel they have a need to *"steal"* your home at a ridiculous price.

If your home is *"priced right,"* meaning not over-priced, or under priced, and your buyers make an attempt to *"steal"* your home by undercutting your price drastically you should consider passing on their offer, rather than negotiating, depending, of course, on how long your home has been on the market and your immediate circumstances. Try not to be persuaded into making a snap decision. They too know how to play on the emotions of a homeowner. They may say they need your decision immediately since, if you are not willing to take their offer, they will purchase another home. Such buyers do not realize that purchasing a home is not a game or a contest.

You need to be very knowledgeable about your home, its location, desirability and asking price before yielding to a lower than expected price to a *"thief in the night."* Selling by-owner puts you in the precarious position of making such decisions without conferring with others.

There may be some situations that warrant accepting a lower offer. Your decision to accept a lower price should be based on factors such as length of time your home has been for sale, your asking price in relation to fair market value, your immediate circumstances (are you involved in a divorce proceeding or other *need to sell* situation), have you purchased another home and time or money is growing thin, is your home in need of upgrading and the lower price reflects this, does your location indicate the need to accept a lower offer, or has the market slowed or suffered in your area as a result of economic distress? These and other factors may contribute to a lower offer than you may have expected initially. I point this out only for you to keep an open mind and to discourage you from doggedly holding out for an asking price that is not realistic. If the buyer's offer is a fair price it would be a shame to pass up the sale over pride or ego.

REMORSE

There is something called "seller's remorse" which is the same emotional volleyball game as "buyers remorse." This *battlefield in the mind* usually develops shortly after an agreement has been reached between buyer and seller, typically after a contract has been signed, sealed and delivered (meaning it's a done deal). It will only compound your frustration, having dealt with what you thought were legitimate buyers, to verbally negotiate a price only to have them change their mind.

Buyers may change their mind for many reasons unknown to the seller. One example is 'buyer's remorse,' a field day of emotional gymnastics that works the same as 'seller's remorse.' Remorse may set in while buyers are making the formal offer or immediately following making the offer. This remorse can be discouraging for a first time by-owner seller or home buyer. Every home buyer and home seller has experienced "remorse" at some point and at different levels.

Once you sign papers don't play the *"we should have asked for more"* game in your head. Save the mental gymnastics for the workplace where there are plenty of other players. Once you agree on a price and sign the papers forget it. It's *finito*! Your buyer may be experiencing the same feelings as you. "We should have offered less, we should have done this or that." Leave the 'should haves' out of your life and your transaction will flow smoothly. If you continue to dwell over what you think you should have done you will find yourself looking for ways to end the sale rather than proceed to close the deal smoothly.

Once you sign the papers to sell your home, if you discover an error or two, or something you promised to leave behind after you vacate, but failed to write down, do not withhold this from your buyers for the sake of saving a buck or two. Once they discover you have reneged on a promise you will be opening up a *can of worms* you will no doubt be eating at some point in time.

86

THE VERBAL OFFER

What would you do, and how would you act if, while walking the buyers to the front door or strolling with them outside your home, they turn to you suddenly and throw an offer your way?

- Would you be inclined to discuss the verbal offer or begin negotiations right there on the sidewalk or foyer?
- Might you be thinking at that moment that the offered price is too low and you'd like to tell them thanks, but no thanks, however, "we will sell for X amount?"
- Should you tell them that any legitimate offer should be put in writing and that price is not the only consideration when considering the acceptance of an offer, and that they are more than welcome to sit down and discuss their offer with you inside the home? Or
- Would you thank them for their offer and tell them to go home, think it over and come back with a better offer?

These questions are raised to cause you to think through a likely scenario before it occurs. A verbal offer is a good way to communicate a potential sale and a great starting point between a buyer and a by-owner seller. However, a verbal offer is **no** offer at all, unless it is committed to in writing. Should you and your buyer begin to thrash out price and terms you would be wise to confirm the negotiations by immediately filling out a Sales Contract. If you sense resistance from your buyer it could be that their verbal offer was their way of starting the ball rolling and now that reality strikes they "need time to think."

When a verbal offer is tossed around like a basketball there is no substance, no commitment. Buyers can change their mind, back out at any time without telling the other party, or be as flaky or wishy-washy as they like since they have nothing to lose. For this reason every state has drafted the same law, **The Statute of Frauds**. Under this statute, and to be enforceable, contracts that create or convey interests in real property must be written and signed by the parties. Once the formal offer is committed to in writing, should there be a dispute, parties to a contract may then seek a judgment ordering the terms of the contract to be fulfilled.

TELEPHONE OFFERS

You should avoid negotiating offers over the phone unless buyers are willing to back up offers immediately with a fax. It is entirely possible that a prospect may call you from home or work after seeing your home. The prospect may have serious intentions yet may want to get a sense of your price before committing so the phone call is a way to *bounce* some numbers off you to see how you respond.

What is important here is not giving in to a buyer who wants to discuss a verbal offer before viewing your home. This may sound ludicrous but it does happen. For example, a potential buyer calls you on an ad from a newspaper or has driven by and seen your 'for sale' sign. From the ad or the brochure the buyer knows you're asking $149,900. This is the qualifier. Your home is well maintained and your asking price is such that there is a little room for negotiation. Other comparable homes have been selling for $148,000 to $149,000 in your immediate area. Before viewing your home the prospect may want to know if you are willing to come down to $145,000. The buyer may even offer $140,000 on the phone as a "feeler." For the purpose of this example, you tell the buyer that $145,000 is very possible.

That evening, or several days later, the buyer arrives to view your home. While viewing your home the buyer turns to you and asks if you would be willing to take $142,000. Now you're offended. The buyer knew prior to coming over that you were willing to take $145,000 (since you intimated you would), but incorrectly assumed you would probably be willing to drop the price even more now that the buyer is *serious*. This game of price dropping is indicative of buyers who **do not** put their money where their mouth is. They are insincere, and do not plan on signing an agreement (unless they get their way with the price) and may call yet again to offer you even less than they did the first time. It is also likely, if you fall for this, they will come back with an even lower price and begin to "chisel" away at your bottom line.

THE VERBAL NEGOTIATION

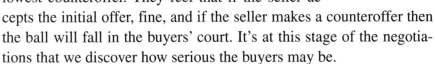

Buyers will often make their initial offer, whether verbal or written, much lower than the asking price in an
attempt to get the seller's acceptance or the seller's
lowest counteroffer. They feel that if the seller ac-
cepts the initial offer, fine, and if the seller makes a counteroffer then
the ball will fall in the buyers' court. It's at this stage of the negotiations that we discover how serious the buyers may be.

The moral here is, *"If it ain't in writing it isn't right."* Don't agree to
or discuss your **bottom line** unless the buyers are in your presence and
willing to sign a contract immediately following negotiations. It is best
to get buyers to make you a formal, written offer. In Section VIII I
discuss how to write the offer and other pertinent information you need
to know when negotiating with a buyer.

If prospects view your home and show interest, you would do well to
ask if they are prepared to make an offer. If they begin a conversation
on price or terms you are free to discuss these but **do not commit** to
specific numbers until they are willing to sign a sales contract to that
effect. **State your position clearly.** Unless they are willing to sit down
and sign a sales contract there is absolutely no point in agreeing to
their verbal offer. They may decide to head home "to think about it."
Then you've accomplished nothing.

I recall several listings where buyers called me on the phone and
made verbal offers on specific listed properties expecting me to call
the homeowners and present their offers without having anything
in writing. After stating my policy on verbal offers many would
either disappear or eventually come to my office to sign the 'offer.'
Selling a home through a real estate office is no different than selling a home by-owner when it comes to putting the offer in writing.
Money talks and *you know what* walks.

Part II

SETTING THE APPOINTMENT

The first and most important item when offering your home for sale by owner is to establish *in house* rules for setting appointments and stick to them, despite any coercing from potential buyers who may suddenly appear at your front door and demand immediate entrance. You will learn in the forthcoming pages some of the ruses and outright lies some would be buyers will use to gain immediate, unscheduled entry into your home. I will show you how to handle such visits. This means you should allow at least a day's notice before a showing, and at a time of day that is convenient for both parties. You may want to take a Saturday morning call for an afternoon appointment. There may be times when you need to compromise and be flexible. Weekends can be such times.

I love those *crazy* calls when people try to push their way into your home by saying they were off work that day and if they could not see the home right away it would have to wait a week. I also love the "phone booth" callers. They just "happen to be in town," found a newspaper and bingo, they want to see your home in ten or twenty minutes and ask if it would be convenient for you. I recently had such a call on a Tuesday, the day my office is normally closed. A phone booth caller identified himself as being from "out of town" (in my neck of the woods everybody is usually from "out of town"). He was upset because he was calling our business line and no one was there to take his call and he just had to see the model home, TODAY or never!

And don't forget the drive-bys. They will stop, grab a brochure, and maybe even knock on your door just to ask a question or two when the answer may clearly be stated in the brochure. They will ask to see your home since they are "here." How does one justify turning down these spontaneous visits? It's easy once you know how to deal with such situations in advance.

There are ways to handle these problems, some we've already discussed. Whenever I leave the Model Home and know I plan to return after Open House hours I leave a note to let visitors know I am sorry to have missed them. I encourage them to take a brochure from the box describing the entire development and ask them to call for an appointment. For callers who insist on seeing your home at the drop of a hat, tell them they are welcome to come by and take a brochure that describes the home in detail, or you can mail them one. And if they are interested, suggest they call for an appointment, or you could set the appointment then.

For those who *drop on by* without notice let them know you would love to accommodate them but it just isn't possible at that moment. If they are genuinely interested in seeing your home they will return. It is typical of time wasters (or looky-loos) to insist on seeing a home for the sake of looking. Such people lack sensitivity and are inconsiderate and give no thought to inconveniencing others.

Once an appointment is scheduled with the caller you should make an attempt to get a first and last name and a telephone number. If the caller is reluctant to give you a last name or phone number you should explain that you need it in the event you need to reschedule the appointment due to some unforeseen interruption. This should be understandable. Don't be surprised if you are refused a last name and phone number.

In preparing for a showing, you need to set house rules for everything, like who will be responsible to meet, greet and walk a prospect through the home. When showing prospects through your home don't hesitate to point out features they may easily miss, especially features and amenities that may not be easily discernible to first time buyers. In an agent listed home it isn't the homeowner's responsibility to point out the home's features to a prospective buyer, but because you are selling by owner it is important for you to take your buyers by the hand, so to speak, and show them through the home. Although showing your own home is not a difficult task this may be new to you since, if you ever had a home for sale through a real estate agency, you probably learned to sit back and watch as the agent guided the buyer around the home.

To Qualify or Not to Qualify - the Buyer?

There are several telephone techniques you can use when you receive calls from prospects who seem interested in seeing your home. First, you should sound very enthusiastic and thank them for calling. After they field a question or two you might ask if they have visited or will be seeing other homes in the area. This will determine if they are new to the neighborhood or have already checked other agency listed or by-owner homes nearby. This will also help determine if they are familiar with home prices in your neighborhood.

You can also ask them if they have been to see, or plan to work with, a real estate agent. This will give you some idea how familiar they are with the intricacies of buying a home. Buyers who have worked with agents may already be versed in certain aspects of a home purchase. It is also very likely if they have been to a real estate office that they were already pre-qualified by an agent and will know the price range of a home they can afford.

It is not your job to qualify buyers just because you are selling by-owner. I realize other how-to-sell-by-owner books offer page after page filled with charts and graphs to help the owner understand how to qualify a buyer. I chose not to include that information simply because it may be confusing to the owner and the task of selling by owner may appear to be more difficult than it really is.

I don't expect you to play the role of a real estate agent or mortgage loan officer. You may not know the true qualifications of your buyers until they approach you with an offer to purchase your home. But you can assume, since they found your home through an ad or by reading your brochure, they already know the price and presumably are comfortable in that price range, unless of course they are dreamers.

Dreamers are those who dream of owning a home and know they can't afford it yet desire to see it anyway. It's difficult to discourage such people from looking at a home. In my mind these folks are time wasters. As cruel as it may sound they have no business looking at homes yet there is little you can do.

Finally, if your buyers have evaded any "qualification" questions, you need to be more specific. You can ask if they've given any thought to the financing arrangements. If they answer no then suggest they contact a mortgage company or bank for a free pre-qualification. You might also suggest they visit the Internet, perhaps in your presence, where there are dozens of web sites for pre-qualifying buyers on-line. When the buyers arrive, tell them you've been in contact with several mortgage companies. Offer the buyer a mortgage guide or payment chart. Be tactful. Questions are best asked in a way that buyers don't feel cornered or put under a microscope, especially when it comes to qualifications.

The point here is to get your buyers to think realistically about the financial aspects of a home purchase. While you don't want to discourage buyers by suggesting that mortgage payments may be too high for them, neither do you want them to ignore the reality of their financial abilities by entertaining unrealistic expectations of how much they can afford to pay for mortgage payments. A buyer may never have taken the time to find out what the monthly payment is on a $125,000 loan.

I get dreamers through my model home all the time who say they want to build a home for $150,000 and have monthly payments of only $700, tax and insurance included, not realizing they will need $60,000 for a down payment to have such low monthly payments. Depending on interest rates, a $700 monthly mortgage payment would only be for a $90,000 thirty year loan, taxes, insurance included (PITI). So for their $150,000 home the buyers will need to come up with a $60,000 down payment. If this is their first home purchase chances are they probably don't have that much in savings. Typically, a second or third time homebuyer will have a larger down payment to work with.

As you show prospects through your home you can always toss in a "qualification" question or two. Learning to field the right questions can reveal volumes of information about your buyers. This will help determine their qualifications, motivation, sincerity and eagerness to purchase a home.

Keep in mind that buyers may lack the necessary mortgage information needed to make a wise decision about what price range to look at to stay within their range of qualifications. Often, buyers go *house-hunting* before going through any pre-qualification steps. Once they discover the home they really want to buy is over their heads in terms of cost, mortgage payments and required down payment they quickly abandon their search. Buyers can be impulsive and sometimes very indecisive. I say this not to discredit the "good" intentions of any home buyer but to point out an all too common reality of the home buying public.

ASK AND YOU SHALL RECEIVE

After walking prospects through your home you may want to ask them point blank, before they leave, what they thought of your home. If they show any interest chances are they will return for a second and third viewing. This is normal and should be expected before they make a final decision. They are probably comparing homes.

The real challenge in talking to buyers, whether on the phone or in person, is being tactful. The point to asking questions is not to discourage anyone from looking at your home who may simply not be qualified but to determine who you need to spend more time and energy with in the event they are qualified. Real estate agents do it all the time. I know I did. Whenever I meet buyers for the first time I let them know my standard practice is to know the mortgage amount they would qualify for so I could then better assist them in locating an affordable home. Some buyers are offended by this. Often they don't qualify for a home because of too many fixed monthly payments, or because of a negative credit history that they ignored. Many home buyers may qualify for the monthly mortgage payment alone, however, after all their fixed monthly debts and new monthly mortgage are combined and evaluated by the lender, using the debt-to-income-ratio, even a good credit worthy buyer may have difficulty obtaining a loan.

I also learned from being in the real estate business that there are buyers who don't qualify to purchase a home at the price range they are looking at yet they may also have had other financial resources available to them they didn't disclose that would have enabled them to make the purchase.

Whatever you do don't ask buyers about their credit history unless they offer the information. This is a private and sensitive issue for many and it is not your role to approve or disapprove their credit standing. Unless you are considering the acceptance of an owner carried mortgage or a land contract, as previously discussed in Section II, the buyer's credit history is immaterial to you.

Some argue that sellers have a right to view the buyer's credit report since they are being asked to take their home off the market for a period of time while the buyer pursues a loan. This point certainly has merit. However, keep in mind, this is a lending institution issue. The buyer's credit report should only be reviewed and handled by those who have the authority to approve or overlook a potential credit problem. A seller should not play the role of a bank or lending institution in approving or disapproving a buyer's credit worthiness.

TENTATIVE LOAN APPROVAL

There is a way to secure the sale, safely remove your home from the market for a week or less, lock in your buyers, and be certain your buyers will be getting their loan within a short period after signing the contract. Specific language can be inserted in the Sales Contract, or Addendum, if used, addressing the issue of a pending, tentative loan approval from the buyers' lender. This method of taking a home off the market for a short period of time is preferred over taking the home off the market for four to six weeks while waiting for the buyers' loan to be approved. You must understand that once you commit to sell, after signing a 'contract', your home will be unavailable to other buyers who may come along so it's imperative to know you have a solid buyer and that the sale will not fall through. There is such a thing as a "back up deal," which is a second written offer from another buyer, but this is difficult to pull off since the buyer must wait to see if the first deal goes through or not.

Typical language in the Sales Contract usually indicates buyers have X amount of days to apply for and be fully approved for a loan. However, they can also get *tentative approval*, which is good insurance for sellers. A *tentative approval* may be based on the buyers' qualifications and credit report only. The tentative loan approval can also be useful if by-owner sellers plan to purchase another home before closing the sale of their existing home. This way, you, as a buyer, can approach your sellers (or agents, if involved) and assure them that your transaction is solid. The sellers (or agents) may be more apt to negotiate with you knowing you have pre-approved buyers for your existing residence. Having the *tentative* loan approval in hand should also help put you in the driver's seat when it comes to working out price and terms. It also tells you that your buyers should be able to obtain the loan without difficulty.

The completion of the full loan process includes employment verification, bank verification of funds, appraisal, inspections, if required, survey, title insurance and other items that may be necessary before the buyer receives a non-conditional loan approval. Since a normal loan process can take anywhere from three to five weeks, longer perhaps if in the middle of the "spring rush" the *tentative* loan approval can be accomplished in a matter of days.

I don't want to seem repetitious but I neither expect you to play Mortgage Broker or Real Estate Broker. There is absolutely no point for the by-owner seller to try to understand mortgage lending rules, ratios, secondary market guidelines or any other type of loan, like one of the numerous FHA insured plans, state insured or subsidized loans, VA, Fannie Mae, Freddie Mac, Ginny Mae, and numerous other financing means and dozens of underwriter guidelines. They're way too cumbersome. All of it may seem confusing and I believe it is unnecessary.

My advice is to contact one or two lenders in your area, gather their information and business cards for handouts and allow them to perform their job for your buyers as the need arises. You may also want to ask the banker, lender or mortgage reps if they work with any particular real estate agent before explaining what it is you want from them. They may tip you off that they refer all buyers to a particular agent or a relative in the real estate business. This is someone you do not want to deal with. They may end up stealing your buyers and sending them elsewhere.

All I want you to do when a buyer comes your way is to make an attempt to find out if they are comfortable in that price range and, by using the aforementioned questions, if they are financially able to make the purchase. Develop your own set of questions that make you comfortable. Write your questions down and memorize them. This way your questions will sound natural when presented. Be creative.

I recently asked a couple who showed an interest in building a new home in my development if together they grossed at least $45,000. When they said they grossed much more than that I told them that was all that was needed to qualify for a loan to buy or build a home in our development for $130,000. Of course debt ratios were not considered for this quickie-qualifying scenario. Using a mortgage payment chart or any handout from the bank as a "qualifying" guide will help. The more you know as a seller the better equipped you will be when it comes to dealing with buyers.

PRESENTATION IS EVERYTHING

Once the appointment is set make certain your home is presentable. Do not take it for granted that the buyer will understand you have children, dogs, cats and *stuff* everywhere because the home is "lived in." NO! They will not understand why you didn't take the time to pick up, straighten up and clean up. They do not understand why someone is in the bathroom when they want to see the condition of the room just because Jan, your teenage daughter, has a date and needs to fix her hair for an hour. They do not get it when they cannot have access to a bedroom because of a temperamental teen that has a KEEP OUT sign glued across the door with other obscure banners. They will never figure out why you locked the dog in the basement and kept it there when they want to see if there are any cracks or leaks in the basement. When you flip on a light switch and the bulb is not working they may think you have electrical problems. Buy a bulb, replace it and test every light and switch in your house. Switches are cheap, bulbs are cheaper. Have a few extra bulbs around just in case.

Apologies should be unnecessary or minimized when showing a prospect through your home. Doors falling off their hinges, or worse, doors that don't close, kitchen cabinets that have broken drawers or loose knobs, windows that won't open or close properly, screens that are damaged or missing, glass that is cracked or broken are all signals to a buyer that the home is not cared for. You cannot change your landscape or the color scheme of the exterior facade but there are many things you can do to the inside of your home to make it "buyer friendly."

Put yourself in their shoes and you may get a glimpse of what is necessary when showing a prospect through your home. If need be you should call other for-sale-by-owner homes and a few real estate agencies and go see a few "listed" homes. Get the feel for how it is done and what your buyers can expect as they tour your residence. Be judgmental as you walk through a home. Compare, and pay close attention to your own reaction if you encounter a home that needs "sprucing up." Your objective is to sell your home in the shortest time possible and sell it for top dollar.

BE PREPARED

You will be asked many questions about your home such as age, lot size, boundary lines, condition of certain components, utility bills, public transportation, utility services such as cable TV, the name of the electric company, Internet access, schools, and many other pertinent bits of information that are important to a buyer to know before making a decision. Again, I emphasize, you must answer honestly.

You should also have proof for property taxes, utility bills, a survey of your property if you have one from when you purchased it, legal description from your deed or the title insurance policy when you bought the home; receipts for the roof, furnace or hot water heater replacement; repair records for the air conditioning and anything else that may be important to share with your buyer.

Buyers sometimes ask about the assessed value of a home. Don't worry if the assessed value (which is usually one half or less of the fair market value of your home) on your tax statement is well below the fair market value. This doesn't mean your home's value is lower. If a buyer questions the assessed value and doesn't understand taxation direct them to the local assessor's office at the city, county or township hall.

Allow them to educate the buyer concerning assessment and taxation.

Be prepared to hand buyers a copy of your Seller's Disclosure statement, whether or not you are asked. The state you reside in may not have a mandatory disclosure law. If your state does not have a mandatory law fill out the form, sign it and disclose anyway. This will appear to be a feather in your cap to any prospective purchaser.

Obtain the Seller's Disclosure form from my website, or from any reliable source, and fill it out completely (to be discussed in Section VI). Buyers like to see in writing any defects disclosed by the seller and they like to see if everything is working properly. The disclosure statement, although not an insurance policy, is a form of a personal guarantee. Any reluctance on the part of a seller to disclose any and all problems associated with a home will appear as a "red flag" to a prospect.

MINIMIZE THE CHIT CHAT

When showing prospects through your home talk as little as possible about personal issues, meaning why you are moving, since this will invariably be one of their questions. For some of you this will be tough. If divorce, separation, neighbors, or anything related to something very personal is the reason you are moving you do not have to tell the buyer. There could be any number of reasons why you have chosen to sell your home. Buyers ask this question because they need reassurance and are comforted to know you are moving because you need larger quarters (or smaller, "the kids have moved out," etc) and not because of the "people next door" or because of some other "problem."

HIGHLIGHT THE FEATURES

Only point out those features they may easily miss while walking them through your home. DO NOT RUSH THEM FROM ROOM TO ROOM. Allow the buyers to guide you at their pace. Open, or encourage them to open, your kitchen drawers and cupboards. Point out the built-in spice rack or lazy susan and sliding drawers. Demonstrate!

Open closet doors for them. Let them see the storage space. This will make them feel comfortable. They may already feel awkward traipsing through your home. Turn the lights on for them as they enter a room. Light is very important. Open window blinds or drapes ahead of the showing. Allow natural light to flow into rooms. Let them see the interplay of light and color that bathes your home. If it's a bright sunny day, rooms can be transformed by sunlight.

You do not have to say, "this is the bedroom; this is the kitchen." They know the names of the typical rooms. You can say things like, "we really enjoy eating at the bar counter instead of the dining room, its so convenient." Or, "our master suite can accommodate a king or a queen size bed comfortably."

As you walk toward the family room you can tell them this is your favorite gathering area for the family, where you sit and watch TV together and play games. Create a vision for your buyers. Help them see the beauty and joy of living in your home. Brag about the wonderful gatherings you've had in the finished basement or the spacious backyard or on the deck. If there is any historical significance to any aspect of your home or its location, like the fireplace being a "Queen Anne" or that some old lumber baron built the home in 1880 then let them know. This will enhance interest in your home.

After you give them a handout or brochure, if they don't already have one, verbally point out what other homes, like yours, have been selling for in the area. Say it *matter of fact*. Don't exaggerate. They will discover these facts on their own. Again, this is where your research will come in handy.

Conversation with your prospects should be kept to a minimum until they take a genuine interest in pursuing the purchase of your home. Although it's important to remain friendly it is also important not to become overly friendly with prospects. Keep your relationship businesslike at all times and your prospects will respect you throughout the negotiation stage and through the closing.

Section VI

How to find the state laws that pertain to selling your home.

This section will tell you HOW to find out which laws are specific to selling your home in your state. It also discusses the intricacies of the "Seller's Disclosure Statement" and the "Sales Contract." [Section VIII will walk you through the Sales contract, clause by clause, where you will learn how to fill one out.]

I begin to explore under what circumstances it *MAY* be necessary to hire an attorney. Many by-owners falsely assume they need one throughout the sales process when they sell by owner since there is no real estate agent there to help.

I further discuss whether or not you should hire a lawyer to assist you with drafting the Sales Contract and whether you need an attorney at all when selling your home by owner. I will describe the utility of attorneys' professional services (not their fees) pertaining to a real estate transaction. I will also give you my honest opinion, based on my many experiences with attorneys, WHEN and if they can be helpful in a real estate transaction, WHEN you can benefit from using an attorney and WHEN it may be important to consider hiring one. This information alone may save you hundreds of dollars, or may save your deal from falling apart.

Note: IT'S IMPORTANT TO KNOW AND UNDERSTAND THE REAL ESTATE LAWS YOU MUST COMPLY WITH WHEN SELLING YOUR HOME BY-OWNER.

Part I

WHICH LAWS APPLY WHEN SELLING YOUR HOME BY-OWNER

If this is your first attempt at selling a home by-owner it is likely you are unfamiliar with your state laws pertaining to real estate transactions. Finding which laws apply to selling your home should be fairly easy. You might begin by asking a real estate agent (if you've already contacted one to help establish the fair market value of your home, as described in Section II.) Experienced real estate agents know which specific laws are applicable in your state.

If you prefer not to deal with real estate agents then contact an attorney for preliminary information and inquire about the relevant laws. The attorney will explain the laws you need to comply with. On the other hand, if the attorney throws a lot of legal mumbo jumbo your way jot it down and verify it with a second source. That's one way to tell if the attorney is just trying to "confuse" you to make you overly dependent as a potential client. I've found this to be common practice with some real estate agents. Their "job" is to convince you that you lack the necessary knowledge to sell your own home so that you will list your home with their agency.

You can also contact your state's commerce department or you can visit your state's web site and perform a search on relevant key words. In Michigan, for example, there are several state and federal laws home sellers must comply with such as: 1) Sellers Disclosure; 2) Well water sample defining lead content, nitrates and coliform (bacteria); 3) HUD "No Lead Paint" disclosure for homes dated before 1978.

AGENCY DISCLOSURE

Each state is unique and has its own laws governing real estate transactions. For example, many states have adopted *"agency disclosure"* laws. Agency disclosure governs the actions of the **real estate broker and agent**, not the homeowner. Under this law real estate agents must inform the buyer and the seller which party they are representing in a real estate transaction. At the time of listing a home agents normally disclose to the seller that they are agents for the seller or *"seller's agents."* This 'agency relationship' means the agent will be working for the benefit of the seller, not the buyer.

It is more common today to find that agents who work with or show homes to a buyer will identify themselves, contractually speaking, as a *"buyer's agent."* These are real estate agents who represent the buyer in a real estate transaction.

As a by-owner seller, if you permit an agent to bring a prospect through your home under a temporary agreement, and the agent makes an offer on behalf of the buyer, the agent producing the offer must disclose his *"agency relationship"* to you in writing, regardless if you are selling by-owner or your home is listed. Aside from this situation, because you are selling by-owner, you may never be involved with agency disclosure. There is much more information concerning agency relationships but since it has no bearing on selling your home by-owner there is no need to elaborate further on this topic.

SELLER'S DISCLOSURE

Many states have adopted a law commonly called *"Seller's Disclosure."* This law states that the seller, in a real estate transaction, must inform the buyer in writing of any and all home defects that are *known* by the seller. The qualifier here is the word *"known."* A seller, after living in the home for any length of time, usually knows the home's defects, including any mechanical malfunctions (i.e. furnace, air-conditioning, plumbing, electrical).

"Seller's Disclosure" is an important and fair law and **must** be complied with whether you "list" your home with a real estate agent or you plan to sell by-owner. Many states have either developed or sanctioned a seller's disclosure form which may be available through real estate association web sites, a real estate association (local board of Realtors), realty offices, office supply stores or perhaps from the state.

You can also obtain this form by calling the real estate agent you consulted for your market analysis, your state's commerce department or real estate division, a real estate attorney, by looking for it on-line on the Internet, at an office supply store, or visit my website.

While disclosure forms themselves may not vary that much from state to state it is nevertheless important for you to check if there are any specific requirements pertaining to seller's disclosure in your specific state. Once you obtain the form, make a few copies, fill one out for practice, and keep one for the final draft. You and other co-owners of your property will need to sign and date the disclosure statement.

This disclosure statement is a preprinted "fill in the blanks," "check box," type form, where each item is answered with either a "Yes, No, or N/A" (not available), offering some blanks where you must fill in your answers such as the age and depth of the well, age of the home, size of the lot, etc.

Under certain circumstances, sellers are not required to fill out disclosure statements. Such occasions include estate sales, inheritance, transferring property to a family member, a new construction unoccupied home, a home sold by a bank or the government due to a foreclosure or a repossession where sellers have never lived in or visited the home they are offering for sale. In these cases sellers simply answer N/A on the form and don't have to disclose to the buyer any information. In such situations, the *Sales Contract* should stipulate that the home is being sold "as is."

MORE ABOUT DISCLOSURE

Your buyers have a right to know what kinds of problems you've experienced with your home, past and present. They have a right to know the current condition of the house and the age of certain components, such as when the water well was installed, when the furnace was replaced or last serviced and by whom, and the age of the roof. Although you may try your best to "hide" certain defects by painting the ceiling with Kilz to mask discoloration from a current leaky roof during the winter months after the ice melts, you must, however, disclose this leak. Your buyers will eventually discover the wet, rotted roof boards, or wet insulation in the attic after they occupy your home and may then have legal recourse if you haven't disclosed this "known defect." However, there are some circumstances where you need not disclose this defect (read below).

The best policy is to be honest. You should reveal the leaky roof problem, when it took place and how it was repaired. It is much easier than trying to hide an old or existing leak especially if your buyer hires an inspection service (discussed elsewhere) that will reveal this defect and others you may not even be aware of. **Honesty is the only policy when selling your home.**

One advantage real estate agents have over by-owner sellers, when dealing with buyers, is they are often in a position of control and can say that homes bought through them ensure that seller/owners have complied with the Seller's Disclosure. An agent can easily *exaggerate* this point by telling a prospect that a by-owner seller may not be disclosing the truth about the condition of a home, suggesting, of course, that there is a qualitative difference between voluntary disclosure statements by the by-owner seller and those elicited through agents. This is not true since all sellers are bound by the law, regardless of how the transaction was consummated, by-owner or agent, and must disclose facts truthfully. By using the Seller's Disclosure statement you will, in essence, be making a *formal statement* to your buyer about the condition of your home.

Flooded basements and foundation wall cracks are always an issue with buyers. In 1987 Michigan was besieged by a "once in 200 years rain" that severely flooded basements. Prior to this rain many homes had never experienced flooded basements. If wall or floor water stains are visible in your basement, and were due to a heavy rainfall or flood telling your buyer you once had a flooded basement during an unusual storm is the proper thing to do. You could simply add that you've never had another flooded basement since, if that is truly the case.

Many new homes with poured walls or block foundations may experience cracks in the walls due to improper curing of the foundation, settling or incorrect backfill material. Homeowners will often ignore these cracks. If you still have a leak but the crack in your wall is not visible your buyers may discover this leak once they occupy your home. If you didn't disclose this defect they may have legal recourse. If this applies to you then you should ask an experienced real estate attorney what kind of recourse a buyer may potentially have. Again, honesty is the best policy and will prevent legal hassles.

PATENT AND LATENT DEFECTS

Typically there are two types of defects, Patent and Latent. A *"patent"* defect is one which may be easily discoverable by buyers, if they took the time to look, like an obvious roof leak where there is visible water damage on the ceiling. Another example may be that the chimney shows signs of deterioration, or the roof is sagging due to age. It should be plainly visible that the roof is sagging and the chimney bricks are falling apart or are severely cracked. If the Sales Contract contains an "as is" clause the seller may not have a common-law duty to disclose the fact that the chimney has cracks or bricks are missing or that the roof is sagging . A seller's disclosure statute or act establishes this legal duty to inform. A seasoned real estate attorney can give you the best advice concerning "patent" defects and whether or not you need to disclose them.

A *"latent"* defect is one that is known by the seller but which may not be easily discoverable by the buyer or an inspection company. An example of this may be cracks along the basement wall, which are not visibly noticeable since paneling has been installed that covers the cracks. This defect is only known by the owner who originally installed the paneling. Another example may be that the roof shingles are very old and curled and show visible signs of cracking or separating, and are in need of replacing but cannot be seen because snow is covering the roof. Courts in many states have ruled that sellers must disclose all "latent" defects to their buyers. Although older shingles, with plenty of life still remaining, may not necessarily be considered defective buyers may inquire about the age of the roof so they will know when it will be time to replace the shingles.

Whether or not a seller has a duty to inform a buyer depends on the type of property, usually a 1-4 residential unit only, meaning a single family residence, duplex, or four unit dwelling. The 'duty to inform' also depends on the nature of the defect, whether the defect is known by the seller, if it may be readily discoverable by a professional inspection, whether the buyer is buying the home "as is," and the nature of any verbal statements made by the buyer or seller prior to signing a Sales Contract. A good real estate attorney can give you the best advice concerning these kinds of "latent" defects and whether or not you should disclose them.

As already mentioned if you have dates and receipts when the roof was replaced and evidence that all the shingles were removed and a new layer installed and any other home repair you should have this information handy for potential prospects. **YOU WILL BE ASKED.** It is vital that you be as accurate as possible.

Latent Defect Example

Many years ago I sold a home where the seller told the buyer in my presence that the roof was 'new'. Since it was winter and the roof was covered with snow the buyer took the seller's word for it. In the spring, after the snow had melted, it was evident the entire roof was not new but patched here and there with new shingles. It was obvious the roof needed replacing. I was asked to testify in court on behalf of the buyer since I was present when the statement was made. The seller lost the case and was ordered by the court to compensate the buyer for a new roof. This took place long before "sellers disclosure" became law.

Don't Guess

Once you obtain the seller's disclosure statement fill it out, sign and date the document. Leave nothing blank. If a question does not apply then put N/A (not available). *Important! When filling out the Seller's Disclosure, if you don't know the answer to a question, DON'T GUESS!*

If you know that your central air-conditioning unit is in need of a charge and it is in the middle of winter when you sell your home you should disclose to the buyer that the AC unit will probably need a service call in the spring. The more they know about such problems the more they will trust purchasing your home from you.

SOME ITEMS MAY BE EXCLUDED FROM DISCLOSURE

You do not have to disclose the age or condition of free standing appliances if they are not part of the home sale. However, if a buyer specifically requests appliances to be included with the sale of the home and they are written in the Sales Contract then you should disclose their condition in writing. In some cases it is best to list older appliances separately on a *Bill of Sale*, instead of a Sales Contract. One reason is that the bank appraiser may need to include the actual value of the appliances if they are mentioned in the Sales Contract whereas the Bill of Sale *consideration value* can be for any amount, even $1.00, and can include any personal items, such as appliances, drapes, curtains, patio set, that you have agreed to leave with the home. Another advantage of the Bill of Sale is that you don't have to state the condition of the appliances, which will eliminate hassles should one of them have a short life span after you vacate your home.

In your brochure or handout for your home, you should make reference to the fact that you have a "Seller's Disclosure" statement available and hand one to every serious prospect who tours your home.

WELL WATER SAMPLE

Another law, if applicable in your state, which is sometimes overlooked when selling by-owner, mandates having your well water sampled, assuming you are not serviced by a municipal well or the city water system. Some states mandate when selling a home, or transferring ownership, that well water be tested to assure the new owner the well is not contaminated with coliform (bacteria from a leaky septic system), and that lead contaminates and nitrates are at an acceptable level established by the state.

You should not try to save a few dollars by taking water samples yourself and mailing them to the state health department for analysis. I would advise that you pay your city or county health department to perform this task since it will look more official and the report can be used later at the time of sale. You can then make copies of the report and share the information with prospects to show them your drinking water complies with current health standards. The water test will also be required by most lenders who offer your buyer financing.

CITY CODE INSPECTION

If you live in a municipality where a 'city-wide code inspection' is mandatory prior to transferring ownership then this inspection should be performed before offering your home for sale. The city code inspection does not obviate the need for a seller's disclosure statement or a home inspection, should the buyers request one. Buyers who are aware of the code inspection report will probably ask if this has been done. A seller who has not taken the initiative to order the code inspection in advance of showing a home will appear lax or unconcerned. The goal here is to be prepared and eliminate all or most of a buyer's objections. We will discuss city code inspections in the next section.

Selling your home should be your objective and in order to accomplish this you should be willing to take every step necessary. City code inspections apply equally to, and are mandatory for, for-sale by-owner homes as well as agent-listed homes. One final thought, when in doubt ask someone who knows.

Part II

SALES CONTRACT

Another form you need to be familiar with is the *Sales Contract*, often called a *Buy/Sell Agreement*, *Purchase Agreement* or *Offer To Purchase*, (sometimes called by other names depending on where you live). These forms can be purchased at office supply stores or other sources, such as the Internet, or through my website (www.how2sellbyowner.com). I must warn you however that store bought contracts don't hold a candle to what you may be able to obtain elsewhere. In the event you require language specific to your city or state I recommend you obtain this form from a real estate agent or a real estate attorney in your area.

Many local real estate associations have one or two generic sales contract agreements where agents merely fill in the blanks. Real estate agents are familiar with these forms since they use them on a regular basis. Because you're selling by owner, perhaps for the first time, you may find the language in some clauses confusing or difficult to understand even though legal agreements today are easier to read than in the past. If you read through the contract and practice filling in the blanks you will feel more comfortable with this phase of the process. Difficulty may arise when specific language needs to be added that is not already listed in the preprinted contract. This can be very tricky and it's at this point you may need the services of an attorney familiar with writing specific language for a clause in the Sales Contract or Addendum.

There may be several types of clauses you will need for your sales contract that are not written in these prepared contracts that your buyer, or you, may desire to include for 'protection.' **YOU SHOULD NOT ATTEMPT TO CREATE OR WRITE ANY TYPE OF LEGAL CLAUSE WITHOUT PROFESSIONAL ASSISTANCE,** unless of course you have experience in this field. Once signed, the contract agreement between buyer and seller becomes binding and can only be changed, altered, or amended when both parties agree and sign accordingly. There are too many court cases on the dockets dealing with trivialities over a poorly written sales contract or a gross misunderstanding due to a poorly drafted sales contract. You have one chance to do this right.

EXAMPLE OF AN ADDITIONAL CLAUSE

One example of an additional clause that may be necessary when selling your home is this: your buyers are prepared to make you an offer to purchase your home and you discover, through conversation with them, that they recently negotiated to sell their home a few days before. Because of this it would be critical to include a clause indicating that the sale and/or closing of your home (include address) is subject to the closing of the buyer's residence, (date of sale and address of their home should be included to identify which home is being referenced), and that the closing of their home must precede the closing of your home. Although this example is not written for the purpose of utilizing this clause for this exact situation (if it occurs) it is important to understand that the buyers may desire "protection" from closing your home ahead of closing their own home, which sold several days prior.

This example clause and other clauses may be necessary depending on your circumstances, or the buyers.' It is also in your best interest, as a seller, to draft language specific to your sale to address any special circumstances. As a seller it is in your best interest to use a protective clause similar to the example above and include an end date for your closing so the deal doesn't drag on for months. This gives your buyers a set amount of time to conclude their business. It would also be advisable, in this situation, to contact the mortgage company or bank processing the loan for the sale of your buyers' existing residence to find out the status of that loan and whether the buyers of that home are qualified before you sign papers to sell your home even with any 'special conditions' written in the sales contract.

The purpose to all of this is to avoid walking into a deal where there are no time limits and no provisions for yourself to *kill* the sale if certain requirements are not met within the agreed upon time frame. This is where an attorney can offer you advice or assist you.

111

Consider this scenario as an example: you show a couple through your home and they decide to purchase your home at full price, no quibbling. The contract is drafted and signed by both buyer and seller. You are very excited over having sold your home at full price. Several weeks later you call the buyers to set a closing date assuming they are ready to close. Your buyers forgot to tell you that they cannot close the sale until they get their money out of their existing home, which sold and is presently going through a loan process. They also neglected to tell you they sold their home to a couple who is hoping to utilize an FHA mortgage plan with a small downpayment which they were hoping to borrow from family. One and half months go by and you get a call from your buyers that they cannot close on your home because the sale on their home fell through due to financial difficulties with the buyer of their home, making your buyer virtually unqualified to purchase your home. Now you've lost six weeks of precious market time, which is impossible to recover, during which you could have sold your home to another buyer.

To avoid this situation you must ask your buyer questions and you must look into every aspect of the purchase, even if it involves checking out the status of the sale of your buyer's home. As a real estate broker it is my fiduciary duty to my sellers to advise them, at the time an offer is presented from a buyer who is awaiting the closing of another home, to allow me to look into the other sale to make certain the deal *on the table* is on solid ground before accepting and signing a Sales Contract. There is nothing wrong with working with buyers who must close their previous home first. The important thing to know is how solid the other deal is before making your decision to sell and sign papers.

ATTORNEY INFORMATION

Contacting a real estate attorney is a good idea before you offer your home for sale, especially if you feel you will need their services at a later date. I suggest you ask the attorney to explain the specific laws of your state you will need to comply with, and to explain the language or legal clauses in the Sales Contract once you find a buyer, if you so choose.

When contacting attorneys be up front. Let them know you will be selling your home by-owner. Let them know you may need their services for specific purposes when and if the time comes. Establish the fees in advance for what you may require them to do. If you ask them which laws pertain to selling your home and they suggest you call back when you have a buyer insist on being informed immediately so you can start your preparations. If they refuse to help hang up and call another lawyer.

If you are uncomfortable with filling in the blanks of the Sales Contract (see Section VIII), then you will definitely need the services of an attorney when you have a firm buyer, assuming your buyer does not plan to procure an attorney.

You will also need the services of a title insurance company to order title insurance (which we will discuss later). Both are listed in your local Yellow Pages. I suggest you make early contact with both to see what information you will need to help your home sale flow smoothly, thus preventing bumps and wrinkles in your transaction.

Attorneys who specialize in real estate can provide important and useful services but, in my opinion, they are not needed during the price negotiation phase of your by-owner sale, unless of course the negotiation involves complex language specific to your sale. I suggest that if you plan to use an attorney for the sale of your home it would be advisable to exclude them from your negotiations with your buyer. That's between you and your prospective buyer.

Attorneys can assist a buyer or a seller in a real estate transaction in several ways. Once a buyer has been found, and a price negotiated, attorneys can draft the sales contract on behalf of the buyer and seller. They can then explain the entire agreement and may suggest the inclusion of additional clauses, depending on the conditions of the sale. An attorney will examine the pre-policy title insurance commitment and may question certain aspects of the commitment or may suggest to the sellers what they may need to do to clear a lien or resolve a "cloud" on the title. Attorneys may even suggest that, as legal counsel, that they appear at closing, which I believe is unnecessary. Sellers, or buyers, can easily collect closing documents days in advance of closing and can have the attorney review these if necessary. It is important to note that the attorney will look over closing papers to assure their clients, whether buyer or seller or both, that the closing documents, price and terms, are in agreement with the terms of the Sales Contract.

It is standard language in every Sales Contract I have come across over the past 25 years that buyers should obtain an attorney to review the title and that the closing is in accordance with the terms of the Sales Contract. I'm certain this clause is there simply to inform prospective buyers that they have a right to obtain an attorney to protect their interest in the real estate transaction.

I have attended closings where attorneys have done absolutely nothing except sit there. I have also attended closings where attorneys have read every word and scrutinized every closing document and would turn to their clients and advise them to sign.

In closing I will offer this nugget: if you are uncomfortable handling the drafting of the contract or attending a closing without legal counsel then by all means hire one to represent you.

Section VII

WHO pays for what?

Buyers and sellers do not always know what costs they are responsible for in a real estate transaction. Not knowing could easily cost you thousands of dollars. I clearly define who is responsible to pay for which closing costs. I explain in detail sixteen separate selling and closing expenses. I also discuss in detail:

- home inspection services,
- city code inspection violations,
- appraisals,
- home warranty purchase plans,
- more negotiating tips.

EVERYTHING IS NEGOTIABLE

It is often said, *"if it isn't nailed down then it must be negotiable."* This is especially true in a real estate transaction.

I recently sold a spec house in my housing development in cooperation with a real estate agent. He brought a prospect through my development just by happenstance. Upon leaving my office the agent asked if I was willing to co-op with his office and pay his company a 3½% commission. I said no, there was no room in the asking price to pay a $4,900 commission and besides 3½% is too much for a onetime showing. As it turned out we split the difference. I paid $2,100 and the buyer increased the price of the home $2,100 so the agency could be paid a $4,200 commission, which fell short of 3%, not 3½%. The point here is when it comes to real estate *everything is negotiable,* including the commission, and seller's and buyer's expenses.

The purpose of relating the above story is to inform you that certain costs and fees which the seller in a real estate transaction is usually obligated to pay, including a commission, if a real estate agent is involved, can be negotiable.

SELLER'S EXPENSES

If you were to engage a real estate agent to list your home the agent would probably provide you with an estimate, at the time of listing your property, of selling costs you would be expected to absorb. This estimate is used to show the seller what the expected proceeds might be, based on an estimated selling price.

Using your estimated selling price, it is essential to calculate your net proceeds and expenses in advance of the sale since most costs and fees are based on the selling price of the home.

Typical seller expenses are:

- Paying off your mortgage(s) with interest through and beyond closing day.
- Property taxes that may be in arrears.
- Water bills that may be in arrears.
- Assessments placed as a lien on your property by the governing municipality, which may be for paving, sidewalks, lighting, sewer, water, and numerous other municipal purposes.
- Property tax and water bill prorations through the day of closing.
- Owner's policy of title insurance.
- Revenue stamps or transfer tax which are attached to the deed at the time of recordation at the register of deeds office.
- Closing fee if a title insurance company is asked to close the transaction on behalf of the lender.
- Termite inspection report.
- Well and septic inspection.

- Code inspection (if applicable).
- Home inspection (if the seller has agreed to pay this expense).
- Attorney fees.
- Commission on the sale.

There may be other seller expenses, depending on which state you live in and what the "norm" is for your area.

Each item will be discussed individually.

1) First and foremost is your **loan payoff**. This is your obligation and your expense. Your lender, or mortgage company, will mail a payoff statement to the closing office so they will have an accurate amount to deduct from your gross proceeds. **IT IS ADVISABLE TO OBTAIN THIS FIGURE BEFORE PLACING YOUR HOME ON THE MARKET SO YOU WILL KNOW WHAT AMOUNT YOU CAN EXPECT TO DEDUCT FROM THE SALE PRICE WHEN YOU SELL.** This figure is important for you to know so you can estimate your net proceeds in advance of selling your home. Keep in mind this gross payoff does not include daily interest charges. Daily interest is collected from the seller's proceeds at closing and usually includes 3 to 5 days worth of interest, beyond the closing date, until lenders receive the payoff funds. If they receive their funds early you may be entitled to a refund of the difference, providing you call and ask. Also, if your mortgage payment is made on the 1st of each month and you plan to close your deal on the 15th, you probably did not make the last payment for fear it would not be received in time to give you the proper credit. In that event you can expect at least 45 days interest added to your payoff balance plus the additional 3 to 5 days of interest for mailing time. Although your loan interest should not be considered a selling expense or an added cost this amount can reduce your net at closing unexpectedly, especially if you have one month or more of back interest to pay. Knowing this in advance will avoid any arguments or disappointments over your net amount.

2)   Delinquent **property taxes** that may show up during the title search are definitely the seller's responsibility to pay. This amount will also be deducted from your gross proceeds at closing. Don't feel your bottom line is dwindling if this expense is deducted from your proceeds. Remember, you didn't pay this bill when due, which should have been paid long ago. So, in a sense, this amount may still be in your bank account collecting interest. You should also call your city or county treasurer to verify any amount still owed and track this amount until paid since it will change month to month due to monthly interest charges.

3)   This also goes for **water bills** that may be in arrears. This is your expense and should be paid prior to the sale to avoid a dispute on who pays what. When too many arrearages show up suddenly at closing sellers may feel they are being "charged too much," when in reality they are only paying bills that should have been paid prior to the sale.

4)   **Assessments** are a different story. If you are aware of a *special* assessment placed against your property as a lien and possibly buried in your property tax statement you should call your city, county, or township village municipal office and find out what the assessment is for. Also find the gross amount of the assessment, the balance of the assessment and the number of years remaining to pay off the assessment. There is a difference in assessments.

Assuming the assessment was for paving a road or for a new sewer project, and there remains a $2,000 balance, there may be a way you can pass this assessment on to the buyer, provided this is done in writing and the buyer is in agreement, and the taxing municipality has no problem with this as well. This special assessment may be used to your advantage during negotiations. (This will be discussed in Section VIII). Knowledge of this assessment and the amount is critical for a smooth negotiation.

It may seem unfair at first for you to pay $2,000 for a road paving assessment since you will not benefit from using the road after you move. On the other hand your property has probably increased in value and has been made more desirable to your buyer because of the paved road. The price of your home, meaning it's true market value, probably reflects this added benefit. The assessment should be discussed as a negotiating point only if your buyer offers you far less for your home than its true market value.

5) **Property tax prorations** is a standard adjustment when closing your home. This is how tax prorations work: For the purpose of this example let us assume your annual tax bill was due and paid on December 1, either through an escrow account or paid directly by you. Several months later you sell your home and are preparing to close on June 1, six months after the previous bill was paid and six months before the next tax bill is due. If, in your area, your property taxes are paid in **advance** (which is more common) then you should be reimbursed by your buyer at closing for six months worth of prepaid property taxes, providing you both have agreed in the Sales Contract to prorating taxes according to this fiscal or due date method. This does not include and has nothing to with any escrow account reimbursement for payment of taxes or insurance, if included in your monthly mortgage payment, which will come from your lender or mortgage company after they receive your loan payoff proceeds.

If, however, the standard method of taxation in your area is that taxes are paid in **arrears**, meaning you live on the property one year before paying tax for that year, then you will owe your buyer six month's in property taxes at closing, assuming you close on June 1. If your annual tax bill is $2,400 then your prorated portion of the next tax bill would be $1,200, or six month's worth. This cost should be borne by the seller and will be charged as an expense to you at closing, though there may be a way around this, which we also discuss in Section VIII.

Assuming you'll be using a Sales Contract, similar to the one offered through my website, one of the paragraphs should address property tax prorations. This is a simple check box and fill-in-the-blank section.

In my area everyone pays taxes in arrears not in advance, which is not a consistent policy throughout the state. You may need to check with your local county treasurer. Often, when I make a sale, I exclude the proration of taxes altogether, depending on what time of year it is, just to save argument and keep matters simple, which amounts to a small savings for the seller and a small loss for the buyer. As long as both parties agree in writing you can prorate or delete prorations altogether, any way you like. This is perfectly legitimate.

It would benefit your bottom line if, should you make certain price concessions with your buyer during negotiations, you consider eliminating tax prorations from the agreement if your property taxes are paid in arrears. Your net proceeds will be higher and you will be hundreds of dollars ahead. Keep in mind the closer you are to the next due date for taxes the more difficult it may be to accomplish this in any negotiation.

6) **Title insurance** is one item you must obtain before closing your transaction. In most cases the lender that processes the loan on behalf of the buyer will order the title insurance. When there is a loan involved the lender will order a mortgage title insurance policy. This is done to protect the lender's interest, which is a buyer expense. At the time the mortgage title policy is ordered an owner's policy of title insurance will be ordered which protects the buyer's interest, which is a seller expense.

Anyone who has been involved in a real estate transaction understands (or should understand by now) that the issuance of an owner's title insurance policy is necessary when buying and selling real estate. Title insurance has eliminated the old

"Abstract of Title" and has fast become the acceptable standard for performing a title search to protect the policy holder (the buyer) against loss from some occurrence that has already happened, such as a forged deed somewhere in the "chain of title."

Needless to say, a title company will not insure a bad title any more than a fire insurance company will insure a burning building. However, if upon investigation of the public records and other material facts, the title company finds that it has insurable title, it will issue a commitment for the issuance of the policy in advance of closing for all to read. Then, after closing, the final policy will be issued and mailed to the policy holder.

Marketable title, or merchantable title, of course, is not necessarily perfect title. Marketable title is what the title insurance company, lawyers and banks seek when a policy is being issued. Title insurance companies often insure over potential defects in title, thus making those titles marketable in most instances.

Generally, a title insurance policy will protect the insured against losses arising from such title defects as, but not limited to: (1) undisclosed heirs: (2) incorrectly given marital status, or mental incompetence; (3) mistaken legal interpretation of wills; (4) misfiled documents and unauthorized acknowledgments; (5) forged documents; (6) confusion arising from similarity of names. If you have any questions concerning title insurance you should ask the title company. You may also ask for a list of what they are insuring or excluding in the coverage.

Sellers are contractually obligated to provide buyers with a policy of title insurance, with or without exceptions, for the gross amount of the sale price, so long as this is included in the Sales Contract. If you have questions concerning "exceptions" ask the title insurance company or an attorney. For a $100,000 owner's policy the one time fee charged to the seller at closing may be $500-$600, depending on the title company and their underwriters' pricing structure. The fee is based on the purchase price of the home. The higher the sale price - the more the title insurance policy will cost. Just so you know your buyers aren't getting away scot free they have to pay for a mortgage title insurance policy identical to the owner's policy, except their policy is issued to satisfy the lender's requirements. This premium is also very pricey and is based on the mortgage amount rather than the sale price.

As a seller you can reduce the cost of the title insurance policy you'll be paying by surrendering your old title insurance policy to the title company processing your sale or closing your deal. The old title policy will be the one you received at the time you closed your transaction (or shortly after closing). You should find the title policy you received when you purchased your home and mail it to the title insurance representative at the title company who is processing the new owner's policy for your buyer. You will see a reduced price for the new policy or a credit for turning in the old one. The credit will be based on the gross amount and age of your old policy, so don't expect hundreds of dollars in savings, unless your policy is recent, like one or two years old.

The Sales Contract will have language addressing the issuance of the policy and the issuance of a commitment for the policy, which should have been ordered before the sale. Once you have a signed contract you need to inform the title company so they can update the commitment and include the buyer's name on the policy to be issued. Your buyer should receive this commitment for the issuance of a policy prior to closing in the event they have questions or concerns or if they want their attorney to review the line item requirements. This will also allow you enough time to satisfy any requirements as indicated in the commitment. In the event you have elected to represent yourself throughout the transaction process you can discuss any title insurance concerns with the title company.

7) **Revenue stamps**, most commonly called *transfer tax* or *"tax stamps,"* is a state and/or county "tax stamp" affixed to the warranty deed at the time of recordation. Since you are the one selling, or transferring title, this expense belongs to the seller. The cost of the revenue stamps will depend on the sale price and the fee structure established in your state or county. In order to subsidize lower property taxes in Michigan, due to the passing of proposition 'C' several years ago, our transfer tax has changed from a few hundred dollars to over $1,200 for a $140,000 home.

8) A **closing fee** is an expense that should be shared by both buyer and seller. The title insurance company handling the closing has a set fee for this service. The closing, handled in the past by the real estate broker or lender, will most likely take place at the office of the title company responsible for processing the title insurance policy. No doubt they will be charging a "closing fee" for their services. This item, although not hefty, should be split equally between buyer and seller. Sharing the cost of the closing fee must be stipulated in the Sales Contract or the Addendum to the Sales Contract or it may be assumed the seller is willing to pay this cost.

In all honesty, if it were a cash sale, a mortgage assumption sale, a land contract sale or any other type of sale not using borrowed money from a third party in the past the broker would 'close the transaction' and not charge the buyer or seller a closing fee. Many real estate brokers today do not want the responsibility or liability of closing the transaction. Thus, they have turned this duty over to the title insurance company to handle including drafting of the deed, the closing statement, and other necessary documents. You would think the broker would pay the closing fee since the listing office, according to some state laws, has the responsibility of closing the transaction. Since you are selling by-owner there is no question a title insurance company, bank or other lender, or attorney, will handle the closing. The responsibility of closing your own sale should not rest on you alone. Seek proper assistance.

9)   A **termite inspection**, although optional or unheard of in some localities, should be considered mandatory for wood framed structures. One never knows if those little ground critters have worked their way into a home. Termites are only one of many wood destroying insect species. The damage they cause is beyond comprehension and can easily go undetected for many years. Usually the seller will be asked to pay for a termite inspection. This burden of proof is normal since it is your home and you should supply evidence to the buyer that no infestation exists.

A termite inspection company usually offers several options for inspection and treatment if critters are found. The fee may be lower if just an inspection is asked for. A slightly higher fee usually includes the inspection and treatment if infestation is discovered. This may be the cheaper option for the homeowner.

Many pre-drafted Sales Contracts used for a residential real estate transaction today have a clause, usually a small paragraph, addressing termite inspection. The language may not adequately cover certain kinds of repairs, the dollar amount or limitation of the repairs the seller would be obligated to make, or who will pay for needed repairs in the event tiny wood eating insects are detected.

If a termite inspection is an issue with your buyer **I strongly suggest using an attorney** to draft an addendum addressing the termite inspection before signing a sales agreement. My concern is that the language in many sales agreements may not thoroughly cover all angles of the inspection, including the sequence or type of repairs that may be necessary if damage is discovered. The correct language drafted by your attorney may save you thousands of dollars and may also save your deal from falling through. The idea here is to lock your buyer into the deal without an "out" should you discover termites or other wood destroying insects in your home, realizing, of course, that you will treat the home, destroy the bugs and make the necessary repairs according to the language in your contract or addendum.

The inspection company will give you and the lender involved a written report detailing their findings and the treatment required if any vermin are discovered. A copy of this report must be given to the buyers prior to or at closing for their acknowledgment and signatures.

Final note: many lenders are now requiring a termite inspection before authorizing the final disbursement of funds. Don't be surprised if a termite inspection is required.

10) A **well and septic inspection** (for those living away from city services) may be required as a matter of standard practice by the lender rather than the buyer. The reason the lender may require this inspection is to satisfy any underwriting guidelines. In most cases the buyer could easily be shown or told by the owner that the septic system is 15 years old, is pumped on a regular basis and is working fine. They could also be informed that the well is a newer 4" with a submersible pump and a pitless adapter or the well is an old 1½" hand driven well with an original screen (point) yet it seems to be pumping fine, is about 40 feet deep and the water has been tested for purity.

In either case the well or the septic may have some problems that could be very costly to repair. For instance, an inspection may reveal the isolation distance between the two, which is a standard code requirement for all new residential systems, does not meet current standards; or that the drainfield (leachfield) may be highly saturated and no longer functions properly; or the well is an outdated system, though it seems to be working okay; or the well indicates that the water has been contaminated. These and other problems are serious and should they be discovered during an inspection you may have to pay for a brand new well or a whole new sewage system. This could easily eat away at your bottom line. It's imperative to have the best possible language drafted into your sales contract, or the addendum, limiting the dollar amount of the repairs you will make to satisfy the sale.

The down side is your buyers may walk if they determine they will need a new well or a new septic system. Their feelings on the subject are different from yours. They are just buying a home. Why should they have to install a whole new system before they move in and where would they get the money after paying closing costs and the down payment? You, on the other hand, who appear to have the deeper pockets would say, "why should I pay for a brand new well and septic system I won't be using or getting any benefit from?"

The idea here is to negotiate this item. If the cost of a new septic system and well is $6,000 you should be willing to pay or compensate your buyer at least half the cost of its replacement, since it was your home and you used the system for the past 20 years. Now it needs updating or replacing. You benefited. Your buyers can easily raise the value of the home $3,000 to cover half the cost since they will benefit from using the brand new system. If presented properly to both parties this is usually a win-win.

In an example of how some inspection problems can be overcome, I recently sold a brand new home to a couple moving from a 100 year old home. They sold their prior residence several times. The first buyer they encountered wanted to finance the home using an FHA plan. Following an inspection of the existing well and septic system it was determined the two were not acceptable to FHA so the deal fell through.

A second couple came along whose parents talked them out of buying the home because of it's age and the perceived potential "problems with older homes." Then a third buyer came along who insisted the county health department inspect the well and septic system. The county inspection report indicated a code violation due to the isolation distance between the well and septic, which did not meet "current" standards. The report also indicated the septic was an old system with a very old fashioned, yet functional, tank. The report also indicated the water well system, a hand stabbed well (verses a commercially drilled well) in the basement was not up to current health standards yet because the drinking water passed all purity tests the buyer accepted the well and septic report and the sale of their home finally closed.

My purpose in telling you this true story is to show the difference between buyers. What seems acceptable to one buyer may not be acceptable to another.

In this next example you will discover the importance of installing a new well and/or septic system, if you have knowledge of either being defective, before selling your home.

I met a couple in my development project who eventually purchased a lot and had hopes of building a new home. They decided to sell their existing home first. Their decision to wait was purely economical. They were more comfortable with the notion of having their home sold and money in hand before committing to a new home.

A little more than a year went by and the couple paid regular visits. Their home, listed now with a second real estate firm, had not sold. I wanted to help them so I decided to pry. I discovered the couple never completed a disclosure statement to give to their agent, who in turn was not able to offer one to any prospective buyers. Their reason for not disclosing any defects was because they were aware they needed a new septic system and a new well. The system had failed and the well was too close to the system to be considered 'legal'.

I strongly suggested that they install both the new well and the new septic system, fill out the disclosure statement, and move on with their life. They sold their home several months later, we designed a new home together, which they eventually moved into.

The new well and septic system was the very ticket they needed to land a buyer. Without it they would probably be sitting on the market for years wondering why no one was interested in buying their home. Installing the new system avoided the negative idea that something must be terribly wrong and thus the issue of cost was no longer a moot point.

11) **City code inspections**. A municipal code inspection may be a mandatory inspection by your local government. If you live in a community where there are mandatory code requirements when selling or transferring ownership you should schedule a code inspection before offering your home for sale and before showing a prospect through your home, so you know the types of repairs that will be required by the city. One reason for this is that informed buyers, while viewing your home, may ask to know the types of repairs required by the city code inspection. Another reason is that there may be some items buyers may be willing to correct after they gain occupancy.

Some repair items may be negotiable between you and your buyer. For example, suppose the code inspector determines that you need to replace several sections of your sidewalk or driveway because of cracks or heaving. In the middle of winter it would be impossible to do this. This item could be repaired by your buyer at a later date. You may consider paying the buyer for this repair up front or, depending on the sale price of the home, splitting the cost and not being involved later when the repairs are made. Or, you may end up agreeing to deduct this expense from the price of the home. These details can be worked out so long as they are in writing and agreed upon between buyer and seller.

After repairs are made and there is a re-inspection the inspection department will issue a 'certificate of occupancy', which most lenders will require prior to closing. As an example, your city may require you to update your old 60 amp fuse box with a newer 100 amp circuit breaker box; replace cracked, broken or heaving cement since they consider this a hazard; replace broken windows, and numerous other items deemed necessary to ensure your home is "safe." The upside to this code inspection is it applies to everyone in your area as well. The down side is some repairs may be costly and you may not be able to afford them until after you close and get your hands on the money.

You should call the building department or code inspector and ask if they will allow the buyers to assume any or all repairs. The buyers may be given a grace period to perform some repairs after they occupy the home and the seller will be issued a temporary certificate of occupancy, which should satisfy any lending requirements. If this is the case you can easily negotiate these repairs with your buyers and compensate them in the price of your home. This will eliminate one more thing you have to do to prepare your home for closing. If, however, repairs are minimal I suggest correcting each item to eliminate one more thing from your negotiations. The simpler the deal the better it is for everyone involved.

12) A **home inspection** is a sore point with me. Since I'm a duly licensed contractor, as well as a licensed real estate broker, I have performed several home inspections before the "rules" changed so I am familiar with the procedure.

Many buyers are unfamiliar with the construction of a home, its internal structure, foundation, roof system, mechanics and so on. I thoroughly understand the importance of having an older home inspected by an outside company who has nothing to lose or gain by performing the inspection. It makes perfect sense for the buyer to include a contingency clause or to utilize the inspection clause in the sales contract asking for an inspection of the property before continuing with the purchase. In many cases the buyer (or buyer's agent) will word the inspection clause in such a way that the buyer has a right to review the inspection report and must approve and accept the report before the transaction continues. A date or specific number of days is always included to allow for the initial inspection so things don't drag on indefinitely.

Once the buyers have reviewed the inspection report and determined that any "repairs" the company has noted are not of a serious nature they will most likely remove the contingency and continue on with the sale.

I **do not advise** sellers to hire their own inspection company prior to a sale to perform an inspection of their home for the simple reason buyers may not believe or trust the company the sellers hired. They may feel you are "hiding" something. It is best for the buyers to choose an inspection company. The language in the Sales Contract should be specific enough, or an addendum may be used to create language, to protect the sellers from having to make any repairs (if the language calls for this) to their home just to satisfy the inspection report at the agreed upon sale price. It wouldn't be fair for the sellers to agree to accept a specific price only to have to turn around and spend several thousand dollars to make repairs or buy a new furnace if the price of the home is to remain the same. It also wouldn't be fair to the buyers to have to purchase the home for the same price they agreed upon knowing the repairs are going to cost them several thousand dollars unexpectedly.

A good negotiation is always a fair one where both sides walk away happy. If this cannot be achieved in the beginning or in the middle of a transaction after an inspection report has been reviewed then one or both parties may never reach the closing.

In the "old days", we often sold homes "as is." This *buyer beware* era, or better known as *caveat emptor* has now turned into, in my opinion, what may be best described as "seller beware." It seems reasonable though to make the seller more responsible when selling a  home, yet, on the other hand, it also appears that more and more buyers today are making more demands on the seller. This shift, as unbalanced as it may seem, is probably due in part to the fact that buyers grew tired of walking into a 'hornets nest.'

As a by-owner seller it is your duty to inform your buyers what defects may exist in your home and to work with them throughout the inspection process so they know exactly what they are buying.

13) Depending on who hires the **attorney**, and for what purpose, it may be advisable for the seller to hire an attorney to read or counter-draft the Sales Contract. I have also seen situations where the buyer and seller have agreed to split the cost of a lawyer to draft the contract agreement and close the transaction. This seems fair except in situations where inspections and repairs are expected to be performed.

14) **Commission** (the 'C' word) is only applicable if you end up working with real estate agents, with or without a listing contract or a temporary agreement, who happen to have a buyer willing to purchase your home and an offer to purchase is drafted, presented and accepted by you. In this situation my advice to you is to negotiate a fixed dollar amount commission due only at the closing. Don't buy into any spiel where agents claim their broker insists on charging this or charging that. You have no binding contract with these agents, unless, of course, you signed a temporary agreement with them to show the home and agreed to a commission arrangement. You may be the one paying the commission but **YOU MUST KEEP IN MIND**

THESE AGENTS WILL NOT BE WORKING FOR YOU OR LOOKING OUT FOR YOUR BEST INTERESTS. THEY ARE PROBABLY A BUYER'S AGENT AND WILL BE WORKING FOR THE BUYER. Make certain this fact is acknowledged before negotiating. You need to be on firm footing with this issue.

Do not accept any verbal agreements from the agent or the buyer or believe anyone about anything at anytime when it comes to a real estate transaction, **unless it is committed to writing**. The spec home I told you about at the beginning of this section is a case in point.

An agent, working for the buyer, who ended up selling one of my spec homes, completely forgot to put in writing that I was to install a Jenn-Air range (a $1,500 dollar item) prior to closing. This was verbally discussed and agreed upon but never written in the final contract. He did remember to include the central air-conditioning but failed to mention the range. Noting this I told the agent not to worry that I would not cheat the buyer out of a range since I agreed to include the Jenn-Air. I did insist, however, that he place the Jenn-Air range on an addendum and have everyone sign the agreement for the purpose of "understanding," in the event of any unexpected or unforeseen circumstances. This way, my heirs, or attorney, in my absence, could read the written agreement and know exactly what was to be included for the buyers prior to closing.

Whether or not you or your buyer are well intentioned it is critical to have everything in writing, and that all parties to the transaction acknowledge any changes or additions to the agreement. This way you avoid any misunderstanding, which can easily happen in any money transaction. You do not want to reach closing only to leave the room empty handed due to a miscommunication.

Although not related to "commission" the previous example is important to understand when discussing selling ethics. This same agent failed to have me sign the proper document granting his office a commission, which I had agreed to pay. I honored the verbal agreement to pay the commission. Eventually, this also was put on paper for all parties to see.

There are many types of people in this world; those who will take advantage of a situation and those who will hold up their end of the agreement. Don't be caught wondering what you should have done differently. Do it right the first time and avoid headaches. The object here is to have it in writing and make certain all parties to the agreement sign on the bottom line. Disagreements and misunderstandings should be avoided at all costs.

15)   The **appraisal**. Banks, mortgage companies, mortgage brokers, credit unions, anyone lending money to a buyer for the purchase of a home, hire an appraiser. The appraiser is someone who has been certified by the state, or someone whom the lender is familiar with (staff appraiser), that is authorized to appraise homes. Appraising a home is not an art, it's a science of facts and figures.

If you are at a loss as to the fair market value you should place on your home and the information you receive from various sources or real estate professionals is too confusing or uncertain then I **highly recommend** you hire an appraiser, previously stated in Section II, to establish your home's market value. Keep in mind once you pay for the appraisal, and although you can use the appraisal as a basis for your home's value, your buyers will still have to pay for another appraisal through their lender at the time of the loan application. There are some situations where one lender will accept an appraisal from another lender. This will depend on the certification level of the appraiser and whether or not the appraiser has obtained underwriting approval status (i.e. Fannie Mae approved).

Your appraisal may become an asset and may be best used by advertising the fact that your home is priced $2,000 (as an example) under its appraised value, if that is the case. You can also refer to the appraised value in your brochure or flier by quoting the appraised price. This information may be the extra plug you need to sell your home for more dollars. The final appraisal will be paid for by the buyers through the lender of their choosing. The final appraisal is not a seller expense.

16) **Home warranties**. A home warranty protection plan is of course another seller expense and is optional. Usually, at the time of listing your house with a real estate agency, you are offered the option of purchasing a home warranty through the realty company. The premium for this policy is not due until the home is sold and closed and is typically deducted from the seller's proceeds.

There are many Internet web sites offering homesellers a home warranty protection plan to offer their prospective buyers. They all sound good. I found several FSBO web sites where warranties can be purchased. I read their hype that buyers prefer properties with warranties over others. There are no statistics that I'm aware of to prove this.

I've never been convinced that home warranty plans are a useful tool for selling a home. I personally believe if a buyer is interested in purchasing a home it wouldn't matter if there were a "home warranty protection plan" or not. I witnessed the birth of the home warranty plan in the late 70's and I've also seen several good home warranty companies fold leaving policy holders with a worthless piece of paper.

Many real estate agents *push* home warranties to convince homeowners that buyers favor buying a home with a warranty. This may be another one of those "industry related" exaggerations. Depending on the area, age or condition of the home, not all "markets" have warmed up to using a home warranty program. Home warranty companies advertise on the Net that home buyers prefer to look at homes with warranties over others. This may simply be an attempt to sell more warranties targeted specifically at the by-owner market. It should also be noted that if buyers in a real estate transaction want a home warranty they can purchase one on their own. You can consider offering this option to your buyer. This will certainly enhance your overall professionalism as a by-owner seller.

What is a home warranty and what does it cover? A typical home warranty protection plan usually covers most aspects of the home, including costly items like the furnace and central air-conditioning unit. When you read the fine print there are limitations to the types of repairs, cost of the repairs, who is allowed to make these repairs, and there's always a hefty deductible. To balance this statement so you don't get the feeling home warranties are a rip-off I have also seen a few home warranty programs make repairs while the home is still "for sale," giving the seller coverage before passing ownership along.

If you believe you can sell your home quicker or more efficiently by offering a home warranty protection plan then by all means do so. If you do offer a warranty to prospective buyers make sure you advertise this fact, including the type of warranty and length of coverage, and place this information on your handout material and website. You want your buyer to know. Check out the company thoroughly and read the fine print.

Section VIII

WHAT to do when a buyer is interested and ready to purchase your home.

Real estate agents would have the FSBO believe they need the agents' expertise, as if the selling process was something grossly complex, obscure, something that only licensed, trained and experienced practitioners are qualified to do. Here, you will discover that this is not true. I give you all the information you will possibly need so you can make a sound decision, sell your home yourself and save the commission (and perhaps attorney fees as well).

In this section I will show you HOW to determine if your buyers are sincerely interested in purchasing your home or are merely *"window shopping."*

- I will also walk you through the steps, paragraph by paragraph, of HOW to fill out a standard Sales Contract (also known as a Buy/Sell Agreement, Offer to Purchase, Purchase Offer or Purchase Agreement).

- IMPORTANT! I cover thoroughly the subject of the good faith deposit (also known as an earnest money or escrow deposit), HOW much to ask for, why a substantial deposit is critical, and WHO will hold the deposit until the sale closes. This issue can be very *scary* for buyers.

- This section also includes more information on negotiating with buyers.

WORKING WITH A PROSPECT

Although buyers tend not to reveal their immediate interest in a home if you listen carefully to their remarks and comments you can often tell if they really like your home. As they tour your home you may pick up "signs" and buying "signals" just by observing and listening.

Real estate isn't magical or mysterious. When a real estate agent takes a prospect through a half dozen homes the agent can usually tell which home the buyer likes. A buyer will either like a home or not for different reasons. It is up to you, the by-owner seller, to approach the buyer and ask. You need no sales experience or expertise to show your home, ask the buyer questions, or discuss the purchase process with your buyer.

When I first meet with new prospects, after a polite exchange of introductions, I ask how they heard about my development or how they found my model home. You should do the same to mentally track what advertising method is working best for you. If asked, I tell them this helps in my marketing efforts. I then give them a brief introduction to our development and the model home before walking them through. I apply no pressure whatsoever. I want buyers to feel relaxed and uninhibited.

One of several questions I ask potential buyers as we walk through my model home is if they are in a position to buy. Buyers usually say that they live in a home and have to sell it first, or they may have already sold their home and are looking to purchase, or they may be renting with a lease that's soon to expire. This information will help me to ask them key questions or offer them advice. I then ask what comparable new homes or new home developments they have seen that they may be considering. I do this deliberately since I want them to compare my new homes with others they have seen. This will be helpful to know. Of course, I don't stop there. I stagger my questions throughout the visit so they won't feel that I'm giving them the *third degree*.

After a complete tour of your home, inside and out, and before they leave, you should ask them if they are interested in your home. This question will inevitably lead to a discussion. They may say they are simply looking. If this is their reply, ask how your home compares with other homes they saw offering similar square footage and features for the same price to further draw them into a conversation. You should also ask their opinion of how your home showed.

The object here is to get them to talk, to acknowledge your home and to give you feedback, what they liked or didn't like. You want them to tell you if they felt your home is something they may be considering. This is good for them and for you. If the buyers are plainly not interested in purchasing your home it would be equally important to know their opinion concerning its condition, value, etc.

If you sense they feel positive about your home your next step is to suggest another appointment to discuss purchasing your home. This can be handled diplomatically by suggesting another visit to preview your home. Buyers seldom purchase a home after only one visit, though this does occasionally happen. It may take two or three visits before buyers are prepared to make you an offer. If they are going on their fourth visit this usually means they're struggling with a decision between two homes or they simply cannot decide. If they bring relatives along on the second visit this is a very good sign. Interfering relatives, however, are another topic that I could write an entire book on.

There are times, however, when a visit by the prospects' relatives could work in your favor. Once buyers and their relatives discover you have all the facts for title insurance, the commitment for the title insurance in hand, seller's disclosure statement filled out and signed, attorney assistance available if needed, termite inspection report, code inspection, appraisal, tax bills, utility bills, receipts for repairs or replacement of the roof, furnace, etc., this will impress them and their relatives that you are indeed efficient, capable and trustworthy. Having these items available eliminates many negative objections or doubts that could arise.

Whatever you do, don't play salesman, don't apply pressure and don't exaggerate the facts. The idea is to create a warm atmosphere so you and your home will stand out in their mind. Once you have created a comfortable environment for negotiating you will be surprised at how willing they will be to offer you a fair price. True value, in a buyers mind, is based on many factors but the most important factor is the condition of the home.

TWO FOR THE PRICE OF ONE

If you are working with two interested buyers at the same time learn to play one against the other. Look your buyers squarely in the eye when asking personal questions and let them know, if they are strongly considering your home, that they should get back to you soon because another couple is also interested and the first one to sign the purchase contract and put down a good faith deposit is the one who will get the home. By mentioning this you will have increased their interest and pushed them further along in the process.

You should also be honest and tell them when the other buyer is returning for a second look. That way you could see them the day before if they like. You need to learn to play this to the max utilizing every opportunity to lock in a buyer. But, whatever happens, **do not** make verbal promises that you cannot or do not expect to keep.

In the event your buyers cannot return on the scheduled day then you could tell couple number one, when they come over, that another couple is returning for a second visit. You do not need to elaborate, explain, make excuses or sound anxious. Just use the facts to your benefit. The goal is to allow each couple to make up their own mind at their own pace. All you've done is add a little fuel. If there is any motivation from either buyer to purchase your home you will be the first to know. A dream situation for any seller is to sit down and entertain two offers from two buyers. May the best offer win!

WHAT TO DO WHEN A PROSPECT IS READY TO PURCHASE

The first thing to do is to invite your buyers to sit down in the breakfast nook or dining room so all of you can sit and talk. The dining area is more conducive for reading and filling out the contract. Ask if they are familiar with a Sales Contract. Let them know the Sales Contract you plan to use is a standard Sales Contract where you simply fill in the blanks. By now, you should have read and practiced filling in the blanks so you are familiar with the document. They may ask you questions and you should, by now, be able to answer them. If you do not know the answer tell them you will get the answer and call them back.

Have a legal pad handy for writing down items to be left behind, or other articles the buyers may wish to include in the final agreement, and for writing down questions that need to be addressed. Give them a blank copy of the Sales Contract to read so they can become familiar with the agreement. If they feel uncomfortable having you fill out the agreement then suggest meeting with an attorney. This will make your buyers feel more secure about the process. However, this also depends on their frame of mind and level of experience. On occasion, inexperienced buyers may be reluctant to proceed with you, thinking you have no experience yourself. It may be difficult for some buyers to trust a by-owner seller to correctly fill out a contract so don't be discouraged if this happens.

THE CONTRACT, FILLING IN THE BLANKS

When you fill in the Sales Contract start at the top of the agreement allowing your buyers to follow along as you read aloud. After reading each paragraph stop and ask if they have any questions then fill in one paragraph before moving on to the next.

Property Description. The first paragraph is usually the property description. Fill in the legal description and address of your home. Have a copy of your recorded deed on hand for reference or your policy of title insurance when you bought and closed on your home. If neither are readily accessible you can also find your legal description on your annual property tax statement. If your legal description is lengthy do not attempt to write the entire legal description in this paragraph. You can simply make reference to the legal description by including language in the legal description paragraph such as, *"see attached Addendum for a complete legal description."* This is commonly done when descriptions are too lengthy for the Sales Contract. Assuming you have your property tax statement it is also helpful if you include the permanent parcel tax number on the Sales Contract or Addendum as additional reference.

Personal Items. The next paragraph in the contract usually deals with personal items that may be included or excluded with the sale of a home. This section should be clearly understood by the buyers. This paragraph, usually written with standard language in the contract, indicates what items (usually fixed to the real estate, i.e. garage door opener, TV antenna, etc.) must stay with the home. However the standard list is usually incomplete. Any of these items may be deleted or crossed off if mutually agreed upon. Please also note the end of this paragraph will usually say, "if any," meaning your home does not necessarily have to have these fixed items.

There should be several blanks at the bottom of the paragraph to fill in things like patio furniture, if included with the sale, specifically mentioning the six foot round glass top table, umbrella, four matching chairs and pads; or items like the 6,000 BTU Amana window air conditioning unit in the living room or bedroom; Amana side-by-side 21.5 cu ft refrigerator; GE slide-in oven/range; all window treatments (drapes, curtains, blinds, and anything else used on the windows); wet bar equipment, bar refrigerator, etc.

Include, and describe as carefully as you can, items your buyers desire to remain with the home. Write down each item. If you run out of room make a short reference to these items in this paragraph and indicate, *"to be continued - see attached Addendum,"* and use the 'Addendum to the Sales Contract,' if necessary, to complete the list of personal items that are to remain with the home. It's very important to be descriptive and clear about items your buyers expect you to leave behind.

[The **Addendum,** a preprinted 8½" x 11" form, typed or hand written, is an extension of the Sales Contract. The Addendum must reference the Sales Contract by including the buyers' and sellers' names, address of the property and date of the transaction. This way there is no mistaking that the Addendum belongs to the Sales Contract. The purpose of using the Addendum is to include a continuation of items, clauses or additional contingencies that may not properly fit in the Sales Contract, due to limited space. After completion of the Contract and Addendum, the Addendum must be signed and dated by all parties involved in the transaction and must be attached to each contract, one for the buyer and one for the seller. Any expenses both parties have agreed to share, i.e., attorney, closing, inspection, etc., should be stated in either the Sales Contract or the Addendum.]

If you choose to exclude items that the buyers wish to remain with the house explain why. For example, you could tell them the dining room fixture was a wedding present and you wish to keep it, the bedroom drapes were handmade by your mother - that type of reasoning. You must agree in writing to replace the light with a comparable fixture or the drapes with a window covering of their choice. Set a dollar amount for these items so your buyers know you won't be visiting a garage sale to replace any of these items. Any items you wish to exclude must be discussed at this point and written in the contract. You should not proceed with the rest of the sales contract until the paragraph describing personal items has been hashed out and completed.

Price. The next section in the contract is usually the price. When I come to this paragraph I look into the eyes of the buyer and very nonchalantly I ask them one simple question: "And what price are you prepared to offer for this home?" (Practice repeating this question until it is memorized). As you recite this, don't hesitate, don't beat around the bush, say it as plain and straightforward as you can in a regular monotone voice and you will get an answer. Your buyers already have a dollar amount in their mind they are willing to offer, otherwise they wouldn't be sitting at your table. Once they tell you their offer, and it seems acceptable to you and your partner, or co-owners, look at each other for a brief moment and give each other the facial "okay," or nod, then proceed to fill in the blanks. No discussion is necessary.

On the other hand, if their offer is much lower than you are willing to accept, or much lower than fair market value, you should be prepared to counter with a price you are willing to accept. You can do this easily by saying, "we appreciate your offer of $140,000 (for example), however, since we are aware of current home values in our neighborhood and we know our home is in outstanding condition we feel anything less than $145,000 is just not acceptable." You can continue by saying, "if you would like more time to reconsider we could leave you alone for a few minutes if that would help." At this point you could leave the room and return in about five minutes. If this time they come up $2,000-$3,000 more and this seems agreeable to you then accept their offer and fill in the blanks immediately before proceeding with the rest of the contract.

If both parties, buyers and seller, are too far apart in price suggest a recess. Tell them politely you need time to think it over. This "waiting period" may be the best thing for your buyers since they may also reconsider and offer you more money next time if they are genuinely interested in your home. During this recess they may go out looking again at other homes and come to realize your home is better than any home in the area and offer you more money on the rebound.

Method of Payment. Fill in completely the method of payment paragraph and cross out subparagraphs that do not apply by running several diagonal lines through them.

If you sold your home to buyers who must obtain bank financing then fill in the New Mortgage clause (if these are the terms of the sale) where the buyers plan to finance 60%, 70%, 80%, 90% or 95% of the purchase price (or whatever amount). Use your calculator to be exact.

You will need to ask your buyers the exact down payment they are planning to make, excluding mortgage and closing costs. This down payment, or their equity, has nothing to do with the good faith deposit we will be discussing shortly.

Filling in the buyer's loan amount is very important in this paragraph since the Sales Contract is *contingent (see Glossary)* on their ability to borrow the designated amount as indicated in the agreement. Keep in mind that their down payment doesn't affect your bottom line proceeds.

Once approved for the loan and at closing the lender will disperse funds to you on the buyers' behalf. You will need to make sure you collect the balance of the buyers' down payment at closing, less any deposit you are holding. For example, assuming your home sold for $150,000 and the buyers put down 10%, or $15,000, they plan to finance $135,000 and give you a $5,000 good faith deposit. At closing, the lender or title insurance company will disperse the buyers' loan amount of $135,000, pay all seller expenses and seller closing costs from this amount and disperse the balance to you. The closing statement will reflect that the buyers have given you a deposit of $5,000. You will then need to collect a cashier's check or money order for $10,000 from your buyers. Altogether this amount totals $150,000.

The title insurance company closing the transaction may want to collect all the money from your buyers including the escrow deposit you may be holding and then disperse the balance of any funds to you in one check. You should discuss this aspect of the closing with the closing agent assigned to your closing. In some states, such as California, money is held in *escrow* and is not dispersed immediately at closing. These funds are held for a short period of time ("in escrow") then released to all the proper parties involved in the transaction after a "holding period."

Your buyers should be clear on the Method of Payment paragraph since they need to know they will have so many days to apply and be approved for the loan or there is no deal. If there is a blank to be filled in for the interest rate the buyer is hoping to get I always include the words *"Prevailing Rate"* in the interest rate section since if you put in a rate lower than the current rate and the buyers end up with a slightly higher rate for whatever reason, this may be used as a legal 'out' for them. Closing this loophole with the words *"Prevailing Rate"* is important to remember, **if there is a place for this.**

Mortgage rates are always subject to change unless buyers "lock in" at the time of application. Rates can fluctuate radically from the time of signing a Sales Contract until closing day. In addition, it's difficult to know what loan program buyers will end up with until they actually submit their loan application to their lender. For these reasons, many Sales Contracts no longer include an interest rate section.

Occupancy. The occupancy clause needs to be handled correctly. If you are expecting to occupy your own home past closing day you need to indicate when you will be out. If you agreed to vacate 30 days or less after closing before your buyer takes possession then you need to pay your buyer rent for the period you will be staying in the home beyond the closing date. Keep in mind that after closing you no longer own your home. You will be viewed as the renter and renters *usually* pay rent. If an attorney is used for the drafting of the Sales Contract a separate rental agreement will probably be drafted covering items like utilities, insurance, care and maintenance including the amount of the daily rent. It should be made absolutely clear to your buyers that you plan to handle their purchase as completely and professionally as possible, meaning occupancy, rent monies, utilities and maintenance of your home after the closing, leaving no issue unresolved.

The 'rent' is prorated on a daily basis, which starts the day after closing and ends the day you vacate or surrender keys. You should instruct your buyers at the time of filling out this paragraph that you will pay this rent the day you hand them the keys to the home, unless there is specific language in the Sales Contract, or it has been arranged with the title insurance company, or attorney handling the closing, that they will hold onto one month's rent and surrender the used portion to the buyer and the unused portion to the seller at the time the keys are surrendered to the buyer or the title insurance company. This is considered the 'norm' since rent is prorated on a daily basis.

Of course, the easiest situation is when the seller vacates the property at closing and there is no charge for occupancy. Although immediate occupancy is convenient for both buyer and seller, it may not be easy to live up to, unless of course you have another residence ready to move into on closing day or have made other living arrangements.

Other paragraphs that have short blanks that should be easy to fill in are: Title Insurance, Taxes and Assessments, Closing Costs, Closing Date, Inspections, Prorated Items, Arbitration and Deposit which are discussed here and elsewhere.

Default. There is a default clause for both buyer and seller to read. It's important for both buyer and seller to understand there are legal remedies for either party, in the event one side changes their mind after signing the Sales Contract.

Arbitration. Nothing needs to be filled in for this clause except agreeing to arbitration as indicated by placing your signature or initials in the blank acknowledging you have read the paragraph. If your Sales Contract does not have an arbitration clause it's a good idea to include one in the Addendum. In the event of a dispute it is much better to arbitrate than to litigate since most states recognize arbitration and will issue a judgment based on the findings of arbitration. Arbitration is known to be swifter, fairer and far less costly than a legal proceeding. There are professional arbitration companies in most major cities. You can also try calling the Better Business Bureau if you need information about arbitration.

Again, let me emphasize, put EVERYTHING in writing. Because lines and space are limited on a typical Sales Contract, you may need to use an Addendum. Using the Addendum will allow you the freedom to list in greater detail things like "occupancy," any personal items you plan to remove, inspections you have both agreed to, how they will be paid and by whom, including any other provisions that may be necessary to agree upon.

Deposit. As you fill in the "good faith" deposit paragraph your buyers should be told that the good faith deposit is fully refundable in the event they do not get their loan under the terms of the mortgage paragraph (above). Typically, the only time buyers are in jeopardy of forfeiting the good faith deposit is when they voluntarily back out of a transaction during the purchase process. Some buyers may not have a clear understanding of the purpose of a good faith deposit.

In some real estate and legal circles there seems to be a misunderstanding of the real purpose of a "good faith deposit," also known as an escrow or earnest money deposit, which buyers put up front as *earnest money* when making their initial offer on a property. Some lawyers argue that without a deposit there is no pecuniary interest or binding agreement between parties. In other words, no deposit no deal. In Michigan at least, it's the signatures of both parties, and not the good faith deposit, that binds the agreement. The deposit is important, but it is optional.

I mention this not to discourage sellers from taking a good faith deposit from a buyer. But you should know that it is the signatures on the Sales Contract which are the binding factor, not the money. However, without a good faith deposit, what recourse will sellers have if they remove their home from the market for four weeks and find out that the buyers have changed their mind and now want to back out of the deal? The sellers would be forced to file suit for *breach of contract, specific performance,* or other legal proceeding according to the law in their state. This will cost the sellers time and money and, chances are, the sellers WILL NOT be able to resell their home until the case is resolved with the first buyers since the courts may force the buyers to close the transaction as agreed. In short, the sellers would have wasted time and money for nothing.

To avoid this disaster it is highly recommended to place in "escrow" a "good faith deposit." Now, the problem with this is three-fold:

How much money should be placed in escrow? Who will hold the deposit and how are you going to convince your buyers to agree to this?

THE SOLUTION

Allow me to share with you a true story before I begin my discussion on the "good faith deposit." About ten years ago I advertised a lovely waterfront home for sale and a couple came along to purchase this beautiful home. I insisted on a deposit equivalent to 3% of the sale price to be placed in my brokerage, escrow account. This equates to about $5,000. The buyer wasn't thrilled with handing over the check but I insisted. In order to secure their purchase without a contingency, they listed and sold their home in a matter of days and did not have to borrow additional funds to close, something they had contemplated doing just in case.

However, during the loan process, I could tell the buyers were beginning to waiver a little. Signals were popping up that hinted to me that, for some reason, they had changed their mind and wanted out but I never brought it up. Nevertheless, we finally closed the deal and at closing the buyers turned to me and admitted that they had almost backed out at one point. I asked why they didn't and they said if not for the $5,000 deposit they would have. They said they could not walk away from that much money. They also said if the deposit had been a few thousand or less they would have walked.

When I entered the real estate business in 1976, on my first day in the office, my broker taught me to collect the largest deposit I could get from a buyer. He said it should be at least 3% of the price of the home, or more. He encouraged me to ask for more and settle for 3%. Being new in the business I didn't quite understand the importance of this until later. With hundreds of closings under my belt I could honestly say I have never lost a deal due to a buyer backing out of a transaction, yet it happens to real estate people and probably the by-owner seller all the time. Why? (see below)

149

BIGGER IS BETTER

The deposit is the single most important item at the time of signing the Sales Contract. In the examples I've discussed I failed to mention one important item. When I recently sold one of our spec homes through another agent I insisted on a deposit of $4,000 but the buyer was only willing to put up $500. I laughed at the agent and jokingly said how I'd love to buy a $140,000 home, any home, and put down only $500 to hold it for a month. After explaining the ABC's of the larger deposit to the agent I then turned the situation around on him and asked this question. Would you take your personal home, worth $140,000, off the market for buyers with a deposit of only $500, knowing that the buyers could back out at any time and walk away from their lowly little deposit of $500 without batting an eye? Would you? He could not answer yes.

I am told it is much easier for a camel to go through the eye of a needle (this is a parable) than it is for the seller of a property to go after a buyer in court to complete the sales transaction. In the event of a default, it is probably much easier for a buyer to sue the seller for *specific performance* due to a *breach of contract*. I was involved in such a legal case long ago where the buyer won the case and the courts forced the seller to close. This was a case where home values increased by the week and the seller demanded more money at closing. Needless to say the buyer was not going to pay more for the home. The sale eventually closed.

PURPOSE OF A GOOD FAITH DEPOSIT

THE PURPOSE OF THE GOOD FAITH DEPOSIT IS TO EN-SURE TO THE SELLER THAT THE BUYER WILL, IN GOOD FAITH, PROCEED WITH THE TRANSACTION AND INTENDS TO CLOSE THE DEAL, AND IF NOT, THEN THE DEPOSIT, UNDER THE TERMS OF THE SALES CONTRACT, MAY BE FORFEITED AND THE SELLER MAY THEN RETAIN THESE MONIES AS LIQUIDATED DAMAGES AND MAY ALSO PUR-SUE OTHER LEGAL REMEDIES AS WELL, IF THE SALES

CONTRACT WORDING ALLOWS THIS.

Although the signatures of both parties are what legally binds the agreement, it is the deposit that keeps it together.

WHO WILL HOLD THE DEPOSIT

In a real estate sale, the deposit is generally held by the selling brokerage firm in a safe place, usually in a non-interest bearing account, or the broker may turn the deposit over to a title insurance company, pending closing, whereas by-owner sellers must convince their buyers to place certain funds with them or a third party. This can be touchy.

In order to secure a sufficient deposit (3% or more) from your buyers and make them feel secure that their money is safe there are two good sources to use for holding a buyer's deposit. Because you are selling by owner I highly recommend you contact a title insurance company or an attorney and let them hold the buyers' deposit *in trust* until the transaction closes. They will probably give you an escrow or deposit agreement to fill out at the time of sale. This may be your best bet to insure a smooth transition at the negotiating table. Your buyers must understand that this money will be returned to them at closing, which they can then use toward their down payment, and as the seller, you realize this deposit will be given to you later along with the balance of the down payment.

In the event you hold your buyer's deposit it is important to note that this money does not belong to you. These funds are not yours to do with whatever you like. You cannot spend this money and you should not draw interest on this money.

Keep in mind that if you are dealing with honest, forthright and understanding buyers they will not hesitate to give you a deposit check payable to you and/or your partner or other co-owners, but this does not always happen. A back up plan could be that you have arranged with the title insurance company to turn over the buyers' deposit until closing, unless you've made other arrangements with an attorney. Utilizing either source is certainly better than losing your buyers over something as trivial as who will hold the deposit. Using a title company or an attorney will alleviate the deposit quandary and your buyers will probably feel more secure.

DEPOSIT MEANS INSURANCE

This is how I suggest you handle the situation as you prepare to fill in the blanks in the deposit paragraph of the Sales Contract. When you come to the deposit clause you should stop and look into your buyers' eyes and explain when you purchased your home ten years ago you placed a deposit of $3,000 in escrow (assuming your home was $100,000) at that time and now the value of the home has increased substantially and you believe a good faith deposit should be at least $6,000. You should also explain that this good faith deposit is your **only insurance**, once the home has been removed from the market, that they intend to close the deal after their loan has been approved.

You should also add that the language in the agreement stipulates that the deposit will be forfeited if they default, meaning that they willingly or voluntarily back out at any time after the acceptance of the contract and prior to closing for any reason except if their loan is not approved. There may also be a default when the buyer has promised in the contract to make an attempt to apply for a loan in a set amount of time and has failed to do so. An attorney can give you legal advice in the event you're faced with this situation. There is no penalty to buyers for not obtaining a loan approval that may be beyond their control. No one should ever lose a deposit if a loan is not approved.

If you sense any resistance to the deposit you should tell the buyers that you are certain they have every good intention of proceeding and closing the transaction and that they have nothing to worry about but that a good faith deposit is a necessary formality in all transactions. This takes the heat off you and places it where it belongs, on them. I do not trust buyers who fumble around and try to convince me a small deposit of $1,000 or less is all they have to put down on a house. I simply tell them they are wasting my time. No way, no how, will I ever take a home off the market for 30 days or more without a minimum 3% deposit.

In most cases, assuming your buyers are sincere, they will see your side of the argument and comply. In the example I gave in a previous section I mentioned a buyer who purchased a home but did not qualify for the loan. The wording in the agreement indicated I was to receive a deposit within fourteen days of the date of the agreement and at the **seller's option,** if no deposit was received I could then declare the sale null and void. I used this *add-on* clause to protect myself from keeping my spec home off the market for a deadbeat buyer who has reneged on sending me their deposit money. Occasionally you may run into buyers who have all their money tied up in investments and who may not be liquid until those investments are *cashed in.* Everyone knows that money talks. When it comes to a real estate transaction this eternal cliché is more than appropriate.

WHO KEEPS THE DEPOSIT

A forfeited deposit, in an agency listed transaction, is handled differently than in a for-sale-by-owner transaction. If forfeited by the buyers, in an agency listed transaction, the deposit is usually shared between all the agencies involved (listing and selling office) and the seller, who may see only half of the amount or less, according to the language in the Listing Contract between seller and broker. In a for sale by-owner situation the seller keeps 100% of the funds if the buyers default on the contract. There is also the likelihood that the buyers may lay claim to the deposit, thereby causing a "checkmate," so to speak, in the transaction. In this situation the seller will need to consult with an attorney.

THE WHAT IF'S

During the negotiation phase if the deposit becomes a real bone of contention with your buyers you should suggest they seek legal council. They may be given advice to place a small deposit in escrow to show their good faith. If this is unacceptable to you then recommend that they place a 3% earnest money deposit with their own attorney. Hopefully, this will eliminate any further objections.

SIZE DOES MATTER

It is my opinion that in many real estate transactions, when buyers make a small deposit (meaning $300 to $1,000 on a $140,000 home), there is a greater likelihood that the deal will not reach closing. It is not only because of the small amount of the deposit but because the buyers may still be out looking for a home long after negotiating on your home. They may be thinking they could easily back out of the deal, forfeit their tiny deposit, and go buy another home and maybe save money. Once they encounter sellers who demand a respectable deposit buyers will think twice before backing out of a deal. Again, bear in mind, should your buyers back out and you choose to enforce the terms of the Contract in a court of law you may not be able resell the home until the transaction with your buyers has been resolved, which can take months. An attorney can offer you advice in this situation.

I contend the size of the deposit does matter. Time has proven this principal to be true.

NEGOTIATE THE RENT

Since you are now aware of your responsibility to pay rent (as discussed previously) to the new owners after closing you may consider using this amount in the negotiations if their offer is lower than expected. For example, if they offer $140,000 for your home when you were asking $145,000, and they come back with $142,500 after your final counter-offer of $144,000, you could tell them that if you are allowed 30 days occupancy, rent free after closing, you will accept $142,500, a $1,500 compromise in price. If the buyers' new monthly mortgage payment is $1,000 or more one month free rent brings you very close to your counter price of $144,000. This is a win-win situation.

Keep in mind one important thing about the rent. The amount the seller is obligated to pay is usually based on the buyers' new mortgage payment including a portion of the property tax and insurance (whether or not this is included in their actual payment). In most cases the buyers' new payment will be much higher than the seller's current payment. When broken down into a daily figure (by dividing the principal and interest portion of the payment, tax and insurance by 30) the gross rent for one month may be as high as $1,300 dollars. The principal and interest portion of the payment depends on the dollar amount your buyers plan to borrow. Don't freak out if their house payment is double or triple what you are currently paying. This doesn't concern you. You should also refrain from making any comment about their higher payment.

Occupancy and paying rent should not be an issue for either party. This is a normal part of buying and selling real estate. If you don't agree with paying your buyers rent after closing then plan to vacate on closing day and surrender the keys. You should not make this an issue of dispute just because you feel you are the owner (former owner) and question why you should have to pay rent. If you don't agree with the concept of paying rent then seek legal assistance.

MORTGAGE COSTS VS. SELLER'S EXPENSES

At some point during negotiations, if your buyers make an attempt at having you pay for this, that or the other, you may want to inform them of your own obligations such as revenue stamps, title insurance and other fees that we previously covered. It helps if they are aware of the costs a seller is obligated to pay. I say this because buyers may feel, due to the amount of *out-of-pocket* mortgage costs they have to pay, that the seller has fewer expenses.

And as a reminder, by the time buyers reach the negotiating table, they should be familiar with their own mortgage expenses as provided for by their lender. According to Federal Law every lender must provide a borrower with a *Truth and Lending Statement* showing estimated costs. These costs are just that, *estimates*.

This is important to know for the following reason: Early in 1999 I was approached by a couple to view a spec home in my development. The price of the home was $129,900. As much as I tried to squeeze information out of them in the first meeting they were not willing to disclose their finances or their planned method of financing until the third time they viewed the home, just prior to making an offer.

Their offer was several thousand dollars less than the asking price. They also wanted me to pay several thousand dollars toward their mortgage expenses, costs that were allowable for the seller to pay (some costs are not allowable). They also wanted kitchen appliances thrown in the sale. As we were wrapping up our negotiations I raised the price of the home $3,000 and guaranteed them I would pay no more than $3,000 toward their closing or mortgage costs. I was not willing to include appliances. They felt insulted that I was increasing the price of the home to offset the mortgage costs. I explained that in some situations where the price of the home is set where there is little or no room for negotiations that this is normal and since they were short the necessary funds to pay their own closing costs this was one way to help pay for those expenses. They didn't agree. They believed the costs should come directly out of my pocket. The lower price, free appliances, and paying $3,000 toward their mortgage costs did not sit well with me. In my judgment this was pure greed on their part.

I then got the idea the next day to call their loan officer. After a short discussion I discovered their actual closing costs were far less than the *"good faith estimate."* Usually, an estimate of mortgage closing costs is always higher than the actual expenses a buyer can expect to pay. The couple had sufficient funds in savings to pay for their own mortgage expenses. The loan they were hoping to pursue was a special FHA plan that allowed them to put 3% down or a total of 3% into the house purchase. This couple hoped I would contribute $3,000 for their mortgage costs so they could keep several thousand dollars of their own money in the bank.

156

I went back to them with one final counter offer and they still felt terribly insulted. My gut instinct told me they didn't understand (or maybe they did) they couldn't go around trying to penalize sellers, coercing them into paying mortgage expenses rightfully belonging to the buyer just because they wanted it that way. In some cases a buyer truly needs help with mortgage expenses. Clearly, this was not one of them.

If a negotiation is one sided you may be dealing with someone who wants everything their way or no way. **THERE HAS TO BE SOME GIVE AND TAKE IN A NEGOTIATION OR YOU WILL FEEL ROBBED.** I encouraged them to look elsewhere.

The purpose of this example is to illustrate the importance of not falling for every line buyers throw your way. If buyers approach you with an offer and need financial assistance to help pay for certain costs, you can deal with that if they are fair with your price. You shouldn't have to come down several thousand dollars, pay several thousand more toward their costs and include personal items to boot. It is perfectly legitimate to go up in price a few thousand, if necessary, to help offset or pay for the buyers' mortgage costs. Also, please remember, although raising the price of a home sounds good to make a sale and to cover all or some of the buyers' mortgage expenses, your home must still appraise at the selling price or it is no deal. Be careful not to abuse this unique negotiating method.

Should this scenario ever happen to you it is strongly advisable to lock in a dollar figure you are agreeing to pay on behalf of your buyers' mortgage costs instead of leaving it wide open (i.e. Seller agrees to pay all of Buyers' mortgage expenses). Unscrupulous buyers can easily take advantage of a kind or unsuspecting homeowner. Be nice but don't be naive.

Section IX

HOW to close your own sale and WHO will perform the chain of title search.

I will show you how easy it is to process and close your own sale and do it with professional help, just like the pros in real estate. You will be amazed how simple it is. I also discuss the role of the title insurance company and the attorney.

CLOSING THE DEAL

Next to filling out the Sales Contract agreement the final phase of the by-owner transaction, once the home is sold, is to *close* the deal. By now you may have already surmised from the previous discussion that closing your own sale is an easy process, which you can "farm out" to a title insurance company. In most cases, if your buyers have contacted a bank or a mortgage company for their loan, you will have little or nothing to do with the closing other than agreeing to a scheduled date for the closing. **YES, IT'S THAT EASY!**

The Sales Contract specifies to the title insurance company and lender the terms of the sale, what to prorate, and who will pay for certain costs at closing. The most important item for the processing of the sale is the Sales Contract agreement which must be completely filled out and signed. **THIS IS CRITICAL!** So long as you correctly fill out key paragraphs concerning occupancy, deposit, prorations and the addendum addressing other cost sharing items, such as inspections, closing fee, etc., you won't have to do another thing other than show up for the closing, review the closing statement, confirm your expenditures, sign the papers and walk away with your check or escrow agreement. **YES, IT'S THAT EASY!**

What may be surprising to learn (assuming you never knew these secrets) is that real estate brokers, their agents, and attorneys all use title insurance companies to process title insurance and arrange the closing. It's a rarity today for brokers to close a deal in their office.

There may be certain circumstances where a broker or an attorney may close a real estate transaction. This may involve a cash sale, land contract sale or an owner financed sale where a lending institution is not involved.

WHAT WILL A LAWYER DO AT THE CLOSING, SHOULD YOU DECIDE TO HIRE ONE?

My most recent attorney involved real estate transaction was a *cash* sale of a 120 acre parcel of land I personally listed and sold. My sellers hired their "family attorney" to review the Sales Contract before signing (even though I walked them through the entire agreement, line by line) and to show up at the closing. It is not uncommon for buyers or sellers of real estate to ask an attorney to review legal documents before signing.

I discovered after reviewing the title insurance commitment (the commitment is issued prior to the final policy and is delivered to the person who ordered the policy for the purpose of reviewing) that there were other co-owners that appeared to hold "title," several of whom had been deceased, but who had not been removed from the "title." I learned as a result of a family inheritance four brothers and their wives were involved as co-owners. It appeared there were two deceased brothers whose families had not probated their interest in this 120 acre parcel of family owned property and their names were still on the title. What made matters even more complicated was that the two deceased brothers passed their interest in the property on to their families through their wills. Everyone who held an interest in the property eventually had to sign the Warranty Deed to satisfy the title insurance company and to release their interest in the property. This fact would not have been readily known were it not for the title insurance commitment.

After a few months we were able to clear all names from the title. I personally closed the transaction without the assistance of a title company. I also drafted the closing statement and the deed. For me, it was no difficult task. The seller's attorney, present at the closing, simply reviewed the closing statement and instructed my client to sign the papers.

I'm not saying this to minimize the usefulness of attorneys at closing. I have seen closings where attorneys actually caught some errors on behalf of their clients. However, for the most part their services can be limited to assisting the seller or buyer with the completion or review of the Sales Contract and reviewing any closing documents prior to closing. The rest may be left up to the title insurance company, bank or other lender involved.

There is a clause in most sales contracts which states that the buyer has the right, or is advised, to hire an attorney at any time during the transaction to determine the marketability of title and that the closing of the sale is in compliance with the terms of the Sales Contract. I believe the reason this clause may be important for some buyers is to prevent a shrewd seller or agent from slipping something past them in a cash sale, land contract sale or mortgage assumption sale when a bank is not involved or a new title insurance policy has not been ordered. I'm sure if one checks court cases across the country one will find law suits against sellers who failed to comply with certain requirements indicated in the title insurance commitment. I'm also certain, in these situations, no attorney was involved.

Although it may be true that people feel more comfortable knowing an attorney is involved it is important to recognize attorneys can be just as fallible as other professionals. In the example above, for instance, the cash sale of the 120 acre parcel of land, several years before finally selling that property, the landowners had approached me to list that same property which I did but was unable to sell. The property was "landlocked" and had no legal ingress and egress. I encouraged them to contact an attorney who specializes in real estate to take the necessary legal steps to obtain a "right of way" to their property in order to make it saleable. I was not made aware they chose to use their "family attorney."

A few years later I was able to list the property again. They showed me a legal right of way easement to allow subsequent owners access to the property. This legal easement was bought and paid for, and granted by one of the neighboring landowners. However, the attorney, who drafted the legal easement, failed to include language in the easement to also allow the transferring of utilities across the easement. I took it upon myself to approach the landowners to sign a new easement, which included language to allow the transferring of utilities (gas or electric) along the easement. They refused to sign. Because this specific language was absent in the easement I was forced to sell this beautiful property for recreational purposes only. Otherwise this property could have been spilt up and sold to several buyers or turned into a lovely development, increasing its value tenfold.

My only purpose in sharing this story is to encourage the by-owner seller or buyer to seek legal counsel who is familiar with real estate. Dealing with the family lawyer is okay for certain legal matters but, if you are uncomfortable signing any type of binding document, without a lawyer, I highly recommend finding someone who specializes in real estate or who is familiar with a residential transaction.

THE ROLE OF THE TITLE INSURANCE COMPANY

Keep this final thought in mind. When a buyer is borrowing funds to purchase a home, the bank, mortgage company, or other lending institution, will be ordering the title insurance. They will review the *title policy commitment* and they will expect *"clean or marketable title"* at closing, meaning the seller is the person conveying title, loans and liens are expected to be satisfied at or before closing and numerous other conditions as stipulated in the title commitment must be removed or satisfied. Whether you need an attorney to assist with your closing is a matter of personal choice. Whatever you're comfortable with should be the deciding factor. Once you read the conditions or requirements as stipulated in the title insurance commitment and still have questions or concerns you can always call the title insurance company (for free) and ask them to explain exactly what they are asking you to do to *satisfy* any requirements. This sure beats calling a lawyer and waiting several days, or longer, and being billed for answers to questions someone else is capable of handling in a more expeditious manner.

Although it is not that difficult to review, understand and resolve any title insurance commitment requirements it is important to note that not all requirements need to be resolved. This is where a simple phone call to the title insurance company will help. For example, a title insurance commitment will not insure the size of the lot or parcel of land or insure the fact that the home lies within those boundaries in the absence of a survey. This is called an 'Exception'. This exception is more than likely going to be resolved once a survey has been ordered by the lender on behalf of the buyer, which protects the lender's interest. The exception should be removed from the commitment after the survey has been delivered to the title insurance company, since that was a condition of the title insurance commitment.

If an encroachment is discovered on the survey, meaning a fence belonging to the neighbor is on the seller's property by 1" or 12" or more, or part of the neighbor's garage or other buildings are on the seller's property, then after this is discovered the title insurance company will probably insure the title around this encroachment, since they are now aware of this. The purpose of the title insurance company is to insure the "title" and not the physical land the title belongs to.

THE WARRANTY DEED

Lastly, if you are asked who is going to prepare the **WARRANTY DEED** don't panic. Get the name and phone number of the title insurance company handling the title insurance policy (which you are paying for) and ask them for a computerized deed (which is supposed to be a free service; it is for me). If they say they will not prepare the deed then you should strongly insist on it since they provide this service for real estate agents, all the time. After all you are the one paying the title insurance fee. The one thing they usually do is they will put the owner's name and address at the bottom of the deed as the "Preparer" of the document. Don't worry. This is normal. If this makes you *squeamish* then ask an attorney to draft the deed.

A Warranty Deed is a simple yet important document that conveys *title* from the seller to the buyer. So long as the deed has the correct names and addresses for the buyer and seller, the consideration value (dollar amount) of the selling price, the correct legal description of the property, the county and state where the property is located, a place for two witnesses and a notary public to sign then the deed should be standard. If the buyer has requested to receive title any other special way, other than title by the entireties, (which is jointly owned property by husband and wife), such as joint tenancy or tenants in common, in order to protect yourself, you must insist to the buyer they approach an attorney to draft the deed. The warranty deed should never be drafted by the owner.

Section X

The Open House myth exposed.

In this section I discuss the pitfalls of the open house and expose its hidden purpose. This information is what many real estate agents don't want you to know. And yes, I do tell all. You will decide for yourself if holding an "open house" is right for you.

- WHAT is an open house?
- WHO benefits from the open house?
- WHAT is the purpose behind the open house?
- WILL your home sell as a result of the open house?

These questions and more will be covered in the following pages.

WHAT EXACTLY IS AN *"OPEN HOUSE?"*

Most people, at some point in their lives, have been to an open house, albeit for a party, a business function, a grand opening event or whatever. In the world of real estate an *"Open House"* event is a blanket invitation to anyone interested in touring a home for sale during scheduled "advertised" hours. An open house advertisement simply invites the *public-at-large* to drop by between certain hours to preview the home. Sounds good doesn't it?

OPEN HOUSE FOR THE BY-OWNER SELLER

The open house is a good opportunity to attract prospects who *may be serious* about purchasing a home and is an excellent opportunity for neighbors to come strolling through the open home. Surprisingly many people choose to stay within the same neighborhood and may buy up, meaning a larger home.

The open house may also be useful when the home has been on the market too long. Buyers who have just started shopping for a home may be unaware that the "open house" home has been on the market for months and will be more apt to visit the open house. This can work for or against the "open house" property.

This can work for you, should you get lucky (timing), because buyers drop in and out of the *real estate market* at random. A couple who may be looking to purchase a home today may change their mind tomorrow. Another buyer who was browsing weeks ago may suddenly jump back in the market and decide to make a purchase. Often, just when you have given up hope of selling, a buyer will pop up out of the clear blue.

If a home has been on the market too long an open house may be just the ticket to attract several fresh prospects. If this is the case then the timing may be right to add an incentive or two and the open house day would be the best time to present the buyers any new incentives.

But, this can work against you if after having your home on the market for several weeks (or months) you decide to hold an open house every weekend or every other weekend. You might savor the traffic generated from your open house but if, after a while, your home hasn't sold the open house may prove to be detrimental. Astute buyers may see this as desperation on the seller's part to unload an *unwanted* home. Because of it's being for sale for so long and unsold they may judge the home to be *undesirable*, as if to say there must be something wrong with the home if it hasn't sold. On the other hand if key words are included in the open house ad, such as 'must sell' or 'relocating,' then the open house ad should draw new prospects each and every time the advertisement appears.

PUFF, THE MAGIC DRAGON

Assume for a moment your home is listed with a real estate agency, and after several weeks you've had one or two showings and little response from the MLS (*see Glossary*) or other advertising channels. Your first inclination is to call your agent and demand an open house.

Why? Because you think that's the magic bullet. For you this may seem to be the "norm." Your home isn't selling, your agent isn't calling and bingo, "I think I need an open house." This is your way of grasping at straws thinking the open house will be the answer when in fact the problem may lie elsewhere. You're assuming, because of the small amount of traffic you've had, that the open house is going to increase interest in your home and a hot prospect will magically come along on that given day. Poppycock!

What may be fundamentally wrong with your home may never be corrected or improved with an "open house." Typically a home fails in showings because of price, location or condition or a combination of all three. The simple hard truth is your home may not be as desirable as other homes for other reasons and will take longer to sell. These reasons need exploring but the "open house" is not the answer. The open house is your own idea to make your home sought-after by someone, by putting it "out there." You're hoping against hope that the open house attracts buyers and that your home is *it* for them. You may think this is what you need to stimulate showings. I'm here to give you the facts.

OPEN HOUSE EXPECTATIONS

An open house may bring you visitors but not necessarily qualified prospects (see the exception to this rule on page 170). No one has control over who will visit the home and who may be qualified or not. When prospects call for an appointment to see your home, outside of the open house, you have a good opportunity to assess their qualifications, to some degree, something that cannot be done during the open house.

A good example of this is what happened recently in a development I am familiar with. A builder, new to the business, built a "spec" home in the development. The home took eight months to complete and he was hurting because he needed to sell as quickly as possible. His bank loan and monthly interest were eating away his bottom line. Since the development was open 5 days a week and widely advertised in newspaper and home magazines, he decided to hold an open house for his spec home on a Sunday. After the open house, he was enthused about having several people tour his open house and bragged about the response. I personally knew two of the prospects that toured his "open house" home. One buyer looked at the home for the purpose of comparison and could not afford the home. This prospect was in a much lower price range, about $28,000 lower than his asking price. The other buyer wasn't at all interested in the bi-level style home, though they walked through regardless. After all, open house required no appointment and no real interest. Yet, these "showings" falsely encouraged him to believe his home is 'hot' and the 'price is right'. In this case the open house did nothing but stroke his ego.

The point here is an 'open house' can give a false sense of security to an owner or an agent that the home is priced right and shows well. Buyer feedback, a necessary ingredient for making a sound determination for the seller concerning price and condition of the home, may not be candidly shared during an open house simply because of the 'open' invitation. Prospects have little invested when touring an open house and may not feel like sharing their honest opinions and thoughts with the owner. Prospects will visit an open house for many reasons, some of which may be difficult to understand.

Showing or marketing a home through the use of an open house is often an act of desperation. The 'open house' is my least favorite home marketing tool (there is an exception to this). An honest real estate agent will tell you that the open house *is not the best way to sell a home,* although it is often used.

You may find that an open house home is being advertised 'open today' along with a new price or an advertisement claiming the price has been reduced.

One sees "Open Today" signs on every other street corner on a Saturday or Sunday and, to be sure, many prospects are ushered through. But the real question is, how effective are Open Houses?

168

WHO BENEFITS FROM THE OPEN HOUSE?

Those who benefit most from a 'listed' open house are the realty agents. The open house is particularly important to them, especially those starting their careers who have no listings and few buyer leads. This is "their day" to meet new potential buyers and future sellers. If they know how to work prospects agents can benefit greatly. The Open House provides dozens of leads for agents since there is the possibility of a future listing should prospects decide to buy and sell.

During open house hours agents are also able to qualify prospects and send them off to look at homes more suitable to their price range or liking. Agents usually come prepared with an MLS book or computer printout of homes for sale in surrounding neighborhoods. Many prospects who come through an open house may already own a home and while they may not be in a rush to buy or sell, they may one day decide to move. As a by-owner seller none of this is important to you since you are not in the business of selling or listing real estate.

The 'open house' was created for the benefit of the real estate agent and also to placate homeowners who may be hounding them to "do something" about selling their home. It is one way for agents to prove they are *trying* to sell their home.

WHAT IS THE PURPOSE BEHIND THE OPEN HOUSE?

The sole purpose behind the open house is to attract prospects, despite their qualifications, to tour the home without making the usual appointment. Buyers love an "open house." It's a good opportunity for them to see what they like or don't like about a particular home. Many of the negatives a buyer may note about a home may never be voiced in the presence of the seller or the agent during an open house. Buyers everywhere know that the open house is their day to look at homes without any seller interference or a real estate agent hounding them with questions or following them around like a puppy.

169

WILL YOUR HOME SELL AS A RESULT OF THE OPEN HOUSE?

You stand a much better chance of selling your home by-owner through other types of advertising and marketing as we discussed in previous sections. The **ONLY EXCEPTION** to this is whether your home is located in a *hot* market area. Buyers who look for homes in a 'hot' or very desirable neighborhood may be ready to make a purchase at the drop of a hat, realizing there are fewer homes that spring up for sale in a specific desired area. **Your open house may be the vehicle to land a fast sale, minimize marketing time and advertising dollars.**

You know if you live in one of those 'hot spots'. If this is the case then you may want to plan your first open house using *banner* advertising and exploit the fact that your home is available for purchase by naming the neighborhood, subdivision or school district. Once your doors are 'open to the public' you will need to be careful which prospect to invest your time with. Avoid the time wasters and those who may be just looking and spend more personal time with buyers who seem anxious to buy. And, be prepared to write the offer (see Glossary) in the event a buyer is ready, willing and able. This is not the time to be shy.

If, while selling by owner, you decide to hold your home open then you should pick a day, typically Saturday or Sunday, when there may be another open house in your neighborhood (especially if it were advertised). At least this way you will get some "free" traffic through your home, which is why you thought you'd like to try an open house in the first place. Otherwise, leave the open house for real estate agents to have their glory day. It would be better for you to focus on taking a realistic look at your home to assess what you can do to make your home more desirable and saleable for the next prospect who calls.

Section XI

WHY do some by-owner sellers "throw in the towel" so quickly and list their home with a real estate agency. And WHY it is some never even consider selling their own home. I also discuss:

- Staying focused (running the course).
- The By Owner helper - brokerage firm.
- The overrated MLS (multiple listing service).

WHY PEOPLE CHOOSE TO LIST

Give me a TV dinner, prepared or frozen food product and a microwave and I'll have dinner ready in ten minutes, or less. I may even use paper plates and plasticware because of the *ease of use.*

Our fast paced society today is filled with people who desire the conveniences of modern living. Many seem to lean toward what is easy these days without giving much thought to cost or quality.

I prefer to cook meals from scratch, with or without the help of a cookbook. In order to prepare a spectacular home cooked meal I must first take the time to look through the vast array of cookbooks and decide what dish I want to feast on. I may even compare recipes to see which one suits my palette. Second I make a list of ingredients that I don't have on hand and trek to the nearest supermarket to buy what is needed. *Fresh* is best. All of this takes *time* and *effort* to prepare one meal, a meal that may last twenty minutes or the memory of which will last a very long time (there is a point to this).

There can be no disputing the fact that listing your home, versus selling by-owner, is often viewed as the preferred, traditional method for many property owners, for numerous reasons. It is much easier,

171

requires less time and effort, especially with today's busy, if not hectic, schedule in the average household.

When we see an agency for sale sign in front of a neighbor's listed home we naturally assume this is the "accepted norm" for buying or selling a home. Many have never even considered the option of selling a home or buying for that matter, without an agent. Why? Can it be because we are so accustomed to the accepted norm that something new and untried, even though selling by owner has gone on for decades and may be more advantageous for us, may seem strange and intimidating? "After all, isn't that what a real estate agent is for," you say?

Maybe the time has come to break the mold and learn on our own, and in the process save a bundle of money. No doubt, there will always be a need for a *traditional* real estate office, despite the continuous rise of by owner sales and predictions that by owner sales will increase by as much as 70% by the year 2010. Selling by owner is not for everyone and is not ideal for every situation.

THE BIG EASY

When you list your home with an agency you are completely removed from having to advertise and market your home, set appointments, show your home, deal with buyers, fill out the sales agreement or arrange to meet with an attorney to complete the sales transaction on your behalf and make numerous phone calls.

HOWEVER, after reading the information in Sections I through X, does the task of selling your home by-owner really seem that difficult? Does the process seem that overwhelming? Can you justify parting with $8,000 to $21,000, or more, in commission fees; money you can use for a new or second car, elaborate vacation, furniture , college tuition or perhaps a larger downpayment for your next home in order to eliminate PMI (private mortgage insurance - see Glossary) which will cost you thousands of dollars. A larger downpayment also equates to thousands of dollars in mortgage interest savings over the life of a loan.

I'm certain after reading this book for the first time you may feel either this is all too easy or very complex. This is because much of this may be new to you. Wouldn't it be nice though to take a shot at trying to sell your own home for several months just to see if you can do it?

While I am encouraging you to sell your own home I am at the same time going to give you some cautionary advice. You need to develop a positive attitude and a firmness of mind in order to see this through to completion. Why? Because you will probably receive pressure to list your home and go the way of tradition. After all, it is easier and doesn't involve any investment, little time and energy.

Consider taking on the task of selling your home comparable to holding a part time job, regardless if there are one or two of you in the household who may or may not work a full time job inside or outside the home. This new part time job may require you to "show up to work" 4 hours one week, 8 hours another week, or 20 hours in a very demanding week. I'm assuming very few people view selling a home by-owner this way.

If you look at the prospect of selling your own home as a business, or a part time job, you will also recognize the monetary benefit for handling your own sale. When the sale is complete you will simply divide the commission saved by the number of actual hours you spent creating your web page, marketing, creating ads and brochures, answering calls, making calls, talking with prospects, and the various other tasks it takes. Do not add up the hours and expense it takes to prepare your home before offering your home for sale and neither would it be fair to add up the hours it takes to prepare your home before each and every showing. These chores you would have done no matter who is handling the sale of your property.

Consider your new part-time job a challenge; a skill you need to acquire; a knowledge you need to grasp in order to bring it all together to fruition. Like any *new* job there will be a learning curve. Once the curve has peaked you will feel more confident with the day to day tasks your job involves. Then, there comes a point, when you will know your job like the back of your hand. Its at this point you may no longer need outside assistance or a resource book (Sell It By Owner and Save). This level of proficiency is when you become more natural in your ability to communicate with a prospect. At this level you will be better equipped to respond to a prospect when asked specific questions you once found difficult or confusing. You also will see how easy the handling of your home is by yourself, without outside assistance.

You will notice your level of confidence accelerate after you've acquired the basic skills. You may even feel a little cocky at times when dealing with a sour prospect or an agent who is overly pushy. **The bottom line is once you learn the ins and outs about real estate you are on your way to selling your home by-owner.**

HOW PEOPLE THINK

On a recent visit to California I met a couple who had just moved from the Berkeley area to the Los Angeles area. They were delighted to find that the area they moved from was a very hot selling market and that their home had sold in only several days. I asked if they chose to list their home or if they made an attempt at selling by-owner. They said they had never even considered selling by-owner. This option never dawned on them. Their home sold for $260,000 with little or no effort and probably no out of pocket expense from the real estate company who handled the sale. This was a one buyer one showing sale in just three days. The couple paid $15,600 in commission fees.

After discussing the option of selling by-owner with this couple I quickly discovered they, I'm assuming, like most people, did not fully grasp the simplicity behind selling their own home. They believed, for no other reason than what word of mouth may have led them to believe, that selling a home required close to a law degree or some broader knowledge than what they possessed concerning real estate and who better than an agent can tackle such a difficult job.

There may be other reasons, or emotional forces, that dissuade you from selling by-owner. Perhaps you witnessed the failure of a neighbor, family member or friend, who, at one time, tried to sell their home by-owner and changed their mind after only several weeks, listed their home, which eventually sold.

It's possible they may have made discouraging comments or had a negative attitude about selling due to some of the necessary things they needed to know but didn't, due to a lack of understanding or interest. Somewhere, perhaps buried in your subconscious, these and other memories surrounding another incident or conversation, seems to influence your decision, all without validity.

Did someone express a statement or make an assertion as to the 'difficulty' of selling by-owner or the "hassle" of putting up with no-show prospects and the bombardment of real estate agents trained to hound, pester and grind the owner to powder until they list? What does it matter! Once you learn how to deal with each situation, before you are faced with them, the easier it will become to continue to deal with these issues as they unfold throughout your selling experience. I say this not to shake you up but to encourage you to think it will not be as bad as others claim. I may even be so bold as to guarantee it will not be as bad as others claim since I believe those who claim they would not sell by owner again never read a book or took the time to become more familiar with a real estate transaction.

My information is designed to help you through each step of the selling process. I've spent considerable time writing each section to insure that my explanations and illustrations are sufficient to walk you through some of the more complex problems you may be faced with. Go back and reread the sections you may be unclear about a second or third time for a better understanding. Once you get a handle on many of the basics I have written you should be able to continue offering your home for sale by-owner until the day comes when a buyer walks through your front door. Assuming you plan to move again one day, whether several years or twice in a lifetime, the by owner experience will stay with you forever and the money you save will be in the thousands.

Run the Course

In contrast to those who never try to sell their home by-owner, there are others who start out selling by-owner with good intentions but soon give up. I believe, once they are actively involved in the process, they encounter *stumbling blocks* or problems and have no clue how to deal with them. They may also be getting conflicting advice from several directions, especially from 'friends' in the real estate business, or experience pressure and end up more confused or uncertain. With no one to turn to for help or answers to some pertinent questions they simply throw in the towel, turn to a real estate agent who convinces them they need to 'list,' which to them now seems like the road to travel.

Remember this: the agents job is to wear you out and make you feel incapable of handling the sale of your home. Learn  to do it yourself and you are on your way to success. After reading this how-to-sell-by-owner-book you should be equipped to handle selling and closing your own home and you will save thousands of dollars.

You should consider going the distance.

The By Owner Broker

Another new idea has sprung up lately, a *'by-owner helper'* real estate office. These brokerage offices typically offer a predefined service for a reasonably low, flat rate fee or preset percentage. Some companies offer placement of the home in an exclusive by-owner homes magazine. They also offer placement on a local web site until the home is sold. For an additional fee they may even assist the owner with the Sales Contract, once a buyer has been secured by the owner.

This type of real estate service may be just the ticket for by-owner sellers who desire some help and limited involvement in selling their home. You may consider seeking out these brokerage firms and decide if they can be useful to you before making any commitment.

THE MLS HYPE

One of many *wiles* real estate agents often use during a pitch with a FSBO is the benefit of the MLS they belong to, known as the *multiple listing service*. This system was designed for members of a local association of real estate brokers and their agents to share listing information across a given market area with other paying members. A real estate office, bank or appraisal firm belonging to this *private club* has access to any and all information about every listed property.

THE CO-OP SALE

A co-op sale occurs when the listing office receives a call from another real estate company showing the listed property with an 'offer' on the table. Together they approach the seller to 'present the offer' and negotiations begin.

This 'system' does enhance the salability of homes being offered through the MLS service since it "opens the doors" to a number of additional agents. However, this **does not guarantee** that the listing office, or the listing agent, will be directly selling their own listed properties. Nor does it guarantee that your home will sell with the help of the MLS (other brokers and their agents associated in the MLS). And, if you are under a three or a six month contract, you are locked in and cannot cancel your listing contract. Then you are out of luck.

The ratios for a listing office or agents selling their own listed property compared to sales obtained through the use of the MLS vary from office to office. Typically the percentages are low. This means there are more successful transactions taking place through the use of the MLS (co-op sales) rather than individual offices selling their own inventory. Another reason for the low ratios is one never knows where a buyer will come from, meaning which area or which state a buyer may be coming from. The listing office, or agent, has no control over who may be showing their listing from a co-op office associated with the MLS. For example, a buyer living on one side of town may contact a local agent to show them a home listed with an another agency on the opposite side of town. When an offer is generated and accepted by the seller, in this co-op venture, a sale takes place and another sold MLS co-op statistic is created. Simply because I was once involved in a large MLS system for many years I can assure you this is a benefit, but no guarantee.

For this reason I'm convinced by-owner sellers stand an equal chance of selling their homes due to the many marketing techniques available today. Since today's home buyers are "shoppers," meaning they like to compare homes before making a final purchase, they will probably come across information about your home at some point in some form of media. Persistence is the key to any successful sale as we have learned in previous sections.

The MLS is a good and important tool for sharing data and information yet agents everywhere invariably assume that thousands of other agents are indirectly working for the seller as a subagent, when in fact **they are not**. I feel it is important for the by-owner seller, and the public, to understand the limitations of this overrated service.

Closing Comments

Should you decide to sell your home by-owner after reading this book, I feel confident, you will give it your best shot. I truly wish you the very best of success in all your endeavors and remember this: there is no such thing as failure if you've made an honest attempt to succeed at whatever you're doing.

Thank you for purchasing, *"Sell It By Owner and Save"*. I'll see you at the closing!

Sincerely,

Michael M Kloian
Real Estate Broker
Residential Builder
Developer

GLOSSARY

addendum A separate document used as an extension of the Sales Contract to allow for more language or additional clauses as the Sales Contract is limited in space. The addendum should be used at the time the Sales Contract is executed, and signed by all parties involved in the transaction. It is attached to the Sales Contract, which should contain a reference to it.

advertising (see also *marketing*) Actual exposure to the public using various media/methods such as newspapers, magazines, fliers, brochures, Internet, or web sites.

agency disclosure Law adopted by many states making it mandatory for a real estate agent to reveal to both the buyer and the seller who it is they represent in the transaction.

amendment A separate agreement, signed by all parties involved in the transaction, adding, altering, or deleting one or more of the written terms in the original Sales Contract. An Amendment is typically used after the initial execution of the Sales Contract as a result of a change in terms.

appraised value (see also *fair market value & market value*) The market value of the property as established by a certified appraiser based on a scientific approach, using current data of comparable or like kind properties that have sold and closed in the past six to twelve months.

assessed value A value placed on the property by the local assessor, usually one half the actual value, for the purpose of taxation.

assessment A specific debt usually placed as a lien, or added to a property tax bill, by a municipality or association.

associate broker A licensed individual equal to a broker, yet operating under the umbrella of a Broker.

attorney, real estate Someone more knowledgeable in real estate law than a real estate agent or broker.

bridge loan Typically an interim loan a buyer needs to obtain, using the equity from an existing home as collateral, in order to proceed with purchasing and closing on another home prior to selling.

buyer (see also *prospect*) One or more persons seriously seeking to make a purchase.

buyer's agent A real estate agent or broker who has contracted with a buyer to work for and on behalf of the buyer.

buyer's market The immediate condition of the real estate climate in and around a specific area where the buyer, in most cases, can dictate or demand a lower price based on supply and demand and other factors.

buyer's remorse An emotional feeling of dissatisfaction with the negotiation or written agreement one has just concluded.

closing The day of reckoning. This is the day the sale becomes final, title is passed and money changes hands.

closing costs Costs or expenses the buyer and seller will incur the day of closing. Closing costs may also be the estimated expenses one may expect to pay at the closing prior to buying or selling property.

code inspection A municipality ordinance (city, county, township, village) designed to enforce certain building code requirements when selling or transferring property.

cold market The climate of real estate based upon supply and demand in a specific region, the time of year or economic conditions.

commission Usually a predetermined percentage of the selling price or a flat rate fee paid to a real estate agency, agreed upon in advance and in writing, for obtaining a ready, willing and able buyer.

comparative market analysis (CMA) A systematic approach typically used by real estate agents to estimate the value of a property using other comparable properties that have been reported sold, usually through the multiple listing service.

contingency One or more legal clauses or phrases, either pre-inserted or freshly written into the Sales Contract, Addendum or Amendment, allowing the purchase or sale to proceed, yet also allowing the option to cancel the sale in the event the contingency cannot be met.

co-op sale A shared sale between two parties, usually two agencies belonging to a multiple listing service, consisting of a listing agency and a selling agency, or a sale between a FSBO and a real estate agency.

counter offer An offer made on the rebound (after the initial offer has been made) by the seller or buyer in an effort to change the former price or terms.

creative financing Specific terms involving a combination of various financing methods, usually involving the seller.

deal, the The end result of all negotiations after the Sales Contract is signed.

default The voluntary failure of the buyer or seller to perform any of the terms agreed upon in the Sales Contract, Addendum or Amendment.

disclosure The voluntary or involuntary act of telling the truth to anyone who asks.

dual agent An agent representing both buyer and seller. This arrangement is disclosed in writing and agreed upon by all parties.

earnest money deposit (see also *escrow deposit* & *good faith deposit*)

The buyer's deposit given to the seller, and held by the seller or a third party (broker, title company, attorney), showing good faith that they intend to fulfill their part of the agreement.

equity The market value of a property, or actual dollar amount what is expected after a sale, less what is owed.

escrow Where deposit money, seller's proceeds from a sale, buyer's down payment, or the actual transaction sits in limbo, until either the closing takes place, or the term or period of time elapses. (The proceeds would then be dispersed to the parties.)

escrow deposit (see also *good faith deposit* & *earnest money deposit*) Usually monies referred to being placed in escrow (limbo) with a real estate brokerage firm, or other third party.

fair market value (see also *appraised value* & *market value*) The price that a knowledgeable buyer is willing to pay, and what a seller, under no pressure to sell, is willing to sell for.

FSBO (for sale by owner) This term, pronounced fizz-bow, is widely used to identify a seller who is handling the sale of their own property without a real estate agent.

good faith deposit (see also *escrow deposit* & *earnest money deposit*) Upon signing the Sales Contract, buyers will usually put down a good faith deposit to show their sincerity about proceeding with the transaction.

greed An emotional sensation one may experience, when buying or selling real estate, which may strongly interfere with reason, during or following a negotiation.

home warranty An insurance policy, or warranty, a seller (and sometimes a buyer) is willing to pay for which covers certain components of the home while the seller is living in the home, and for a specified period of time, after the buyer occupies the home.

hot market A specific time of year, or a specific region or neighborhood where the real estate market is very good (normally properties sell quickly with or without an agent), due to many factors.

land contract A form of owner financing, not involving traditional lending methods, where title is not passed until the land contract is paid in full.

latent defect A defect that may not be readily discernible or noticeable without prior knowledge or an inspection, i.e. a leaky roof that was not repaired and any resulting well hidden damage.

listing contract An agreement, between the seller of a property and the brokerage firm, defining price, terms, amount of commission, and the length of time the contract will be in force.

looky-loo A 70's term coined to describe one or more persons looking to make a purchase yet may not have any intention of buying due to a lack of motivation. They also enjoy looking at home after home strictly for the fun of it or for ideas.

marketing (see also *advertising*) The term used when one is offering one's property for sale, using various means and methods of advertising and exposure.

market conditions The current status of the real estate market as a whole (varies by locale), which is usually affected by interest rates, the health of the economy and unemployment.

market value (see also *fair market value* & *appraised value*) The price one may expect to sell for; based on current market conditions and what other comparable properties are selling for in the immediate area.

MLS (Multiple Listing Service) A private service used primarily by members of real estate agencies within a given geographic area. The members share information with each other concerning every property that is listed, and sold, by the members who belong to the system.

mortgage costs Actual expenses a buyer can expect to pay for obtaining a loan, usually paid at the closing, with some costs paid up front.

negotiations The verbal or written transformation of wants and wishes.

offer A formal written agreement expressing the desires of the one making the offer with reference to price, terms and conditions of the sale. The offer, when signed by all parties to the transaction, becomes binding.

Open House A specific day when a home is advertised as open to the public.

patent defect A defect that may be noticeable if one were to just look, i.e. bricks falling down or the roof is sagging.

points Money paid to a lender based on the loan amount (one point equals one percent of the mortgage) which increases the yield or value of the loan.

PMI (private mortgage insurance) An insurance policy obtained by the lender, on behalf of the buyer, to insure a portion of the loan to the lender, in the event of default. PMI is required by conventional underwriters for mortgage loans less than 20% down. A premium is paid for at the closing and a percentage, usually ¼% is added to the monthly payment until 20% equity has been achieved.

pre-approved buyer (see also *qualified buyer*) A prospect who has obtained a pre-approval from a lender, for a specific loan amount, usually in writing. This letter of approval may be presented to the seller or a real estate agent as evidence of a loan pre-approval.

price Either the agreed upon sale price derived through negotiations, or the asking price of a property for sale as established by the seller.

pro-ration A mathematical equation for calculating certain costs or expenses usually broken down by a per diem (per day) usage, i.e.

water bills prorated over a thirty day period.

prospect (see also *buyer*) One or more persons seeking to make a purchase.

purchase money mortgage A mortgage granted by the seller to the buyer to assist with financing a portion of the down payment.

qualified buyer A prospect who has been pre-qualified by a lender prior to searching for a property. They know how much they need for the required down payment (they have the monies available to them in savings), they know what to expect for a monthly payment, and short of finding the right property, they are ready to proceed.

real estate agent A licensed individual who presents one's self to the public as being both knowledgeable and professional. A real estate agent, or licensee, must work under the umbrella of a broker.

real estate broker A licensed individual, usually the head of a real estate office or firm, possessing more education and knowledge than a real estate agent. The broker is the ultimate responsible person.

real estate Typically any real property where title may be transferred: Vacant land, home, duplex, condominium, vacation home, or any real estate in general.

REALTOR This term applies only to real estate people who are members of the National Association of REALTORS. Membership implies a higher form of ethics and professionalism.

revenue stamps (see also *transfer tax*) Stamps that are affixed to the Warranty Deed at the time of recordation. The cost of the stamps is based on the transfer amount or selling price and is paid to the local County Register of Deeds.

Sales Contract A very lengthy, legal, and binding document, usually preprinted using a fill-in-the-blank format, expressing price, terms and conditions of the parties involved in the transaction. It is comprised of all the necessary language it takes for the buyer and seller to come to a meeting of the minds. This contract is also referred to as a Purchase Agreement, Purchase Offer, Offer to Purchase, Sales Agreement, Buy/Sell Agreement (and probably several other names).

sellers agent A real estate agent or broker who has contracted with the seller to work for, and on behalf of, the seller. A level of fiduciary (trust) is a given when obtaining a listing contract.

seller's disclosure A law, adopted by many states, making it mandatory for the seller to reveal to the buyer, in writing, prior to the acceptance of an offer, the current condition of the property and any defects that are known by the seller.

seller's market The immediate condition of the real estate climate in and around a specific area where the seller (in most cases) can dictate or demand a higher price or better terms, based on desirability of location, supply and demand, and other factors.

sellers remorse An emotional feeling of dissatisfaction with the negotiation or written agreement one has just concluded.

selling costs Actual expenses a seller can expect to pay on the day of closing, usually deducted from the sellers proceeds.

Statute of Frauds A law that indicates all real estate transactions must be reduced to writing and signed by all parties to the transaction.

survey A measurement and location of the boundary of a parcel of real estate.

termination of agreement A document used to cancel or kill a deal, which is signed by all parties involved in the transaction.

186

terms Specific terms of the sale, i.e. cash, contract, new mortgage, owner financing, and any other circumstances surrounding the sale.

title company A title insurance company whose function is to provide a title search in order to establish positive ownership, liens and anything else that may be recorded. They are responsible for issuing the owner's title insurance policy issued to the buyer on behalf of the seller, mortgage title insurance issued to the lender on behalf of the buyer, escrow and closing services.

title insurance A policy of insurance issued to the buyer by a title company, insuring the title, or marketability of the title, after performing an extensive search of the history of that title.

title insurance commitment A pre-policy commitment issued prior to the closing in order for all to examine. Once all of the requirements have been met as stated on the commitment, the title company will issue a final title insurance policy following the closing.

TLC (tender loving care) Usually a property that is suffering from neglect or needs extra maintenance and repairs.

transaction coordinator An individual handling a real estate transaction who works for neither the buyer nor the seller and who should refrain from offering any advice since they are considered a neutral party.

transfer tax (see also *revenue stamps*) This tax is paid to the county and/or state of residence when transferring property from the current owner to the new owner and is based on the selling price.

underwriter An unknown third party who establishes guidelines and ever changing rules for lenders to follow in order to comply with certain standards in preparation of the loan to be sold.

verbal agreement A nonbinding oral discussion, sometimes prior to the written agreement, expressing the desires of the parties.

Index

FREE FORMS

To qualify for free forms you must be the original purchaser of a printed version of *"Sell It By Owner and Save"*. You are entitled to one complete set of very useful and professional real estate forms including a Sales Contract specifically designed for the by-owner.

Simply e-mail the publisher at:
freeforms@how2sellbyowner.com

Tell us where and when you purchased the book and the price you paid. The Publisher will send your forms to any **one** e-mail address you supply.

Ten forms, a total of 17 pages, will be delivered by **e-mail** in PDF file format, perfectly formatted for 8 1/2 x 11 paper, ready for your printer. You will need Adobe Acrobat Reader, a **free** program from adobe.com. Most computer systems already have Acrobat Reader installed. The PDF file will automatically open once you point and click.

You can visit our web site at: www.how2sellbyowner.com, for a complete description of the contract & forms. These real estate documents have been rated the very best forms ever offered to the public and they are free so long as you purchased out title. One customer, a retired real estate agent, claims these forms are the same forms real estate agents use every day to complete or make a sale.

The forms are complimentary. There is no charge.

ORDER FORM

Order "Sell It By Owner and Save" for a friend, relative or someone you know that will benefit from selling by owner and save thousands of dollars in commission fees, just like you. They will probably appreciate the gesture and maybe compensate you for your kindness (after they pocket thousands of dollars in saved commissions).

Carefully remove this page from this book, complete the form below and send this along with your payment of $19.95 per book to:

HOW TO LLC
PO BOX 53
HOWARD CITY, MI 49329

USPS MEDIA MAIL INCLUDED (4 - 8 days) SHIPPING

MICHIGAN RESIDENTS MUST ADD $1.08 in Sales Tax

_____
name

_____
shipping/mailing address

_____
city/state/zip

_____
phone number   /   e-mail address

_____
number of books x $19.95   =

www.sellitbyownerandsave.com